THE MORNINGSIDE MODEL OF GENERATIVE INSTRUCTION: WHAT IT MEANS TO LEAVE NO CHILD BEHIND

Kent Johnson, Ph.D[1]
Founder and Director, Morningside Academy
Seattle, Washington

Elizabeth M. Street, Ed.D
Professor of Psychology, Central Washington University
Ellensburg, Washington

With contributions from Susan Malmquist
and Joanne Robbins

---

[1]Authorship is considered to be equal.

Published by the Cambridge Center for Behavioral Studies

336 Baker Avenue
Concord, MA 01742 USA
(978) 369-2227
www.behavior.org

ISBN: 1-881317-15-3

TABLE OF CONTENTS

ABOUT THE AUTHORS

Dr. Kent Johnson founded Morningside Academy, in Seattle, Washington, in 1980, and currently serves as its Executive Director. Morningside is a laboratory school for elementary and middle school children and youth. Morningside investigates effective curriculum materials and teaching methods, and has provided training and consulting in instruction to over 80 schools and agencies throughout the USA and Canada since 1991.

Dr. Johnson has served in all the positions at Morningside, including classroom teacher for 10 years, financial manager, administrator, teacher trainer, school psychologist, teacher trainer, and school consultant. He has published several seminal papers about the Morningside Model of Generative Instruction: A general framework for teaching and a blend of research-based curriculum and teaching methods. The Morningside Model focuses upon foundation skills in reading, writing, mathematics, thinking, reasoning, problem solving, studying core content, and project-based learning. Over 17,000 students and over a thousand teachers have used the Morningside Model of Generative Instruction.

Dr. Johnson is also co-founder of Headsprout, Inc., which produces web-based, interactive, cartoon-driven instructional programs in reading, math, and other foundations skills. Its first product, Headsprout Reading, for children aged 4 to 6 years, is now available at http://www.headsprout.com.

Dr. Elizabeth Street is Professor of Psychology and Executive Assistant to the President at Central Washington University. Her areas of expertise include learning, development, and educational psychology with an emphasis in curriculum design, instructional strategies, assessment, and behavior analysis. During her 25-year tenure as professor of

1

psychology at Central Washington University, she has been a member of the institution's Center for Teaching and Learning and has been actively involved in the preparation of teachers. She is an ardent supporter of scientifically-based instructional practices.

During the 1994–1995 academic year, Dr. Street served as a Congressional Science Fellow under the auspices of the American Psychological Association in the Labor and Human Resources Committee Office of Senator Edward M. Kennedy.

Dr. Street has been associated with Morningside Academy since its founding. She has served on the Board of Directors, spent a summer teaching in the Morningside Academy laboratory school, has been a faculty member for Morningside's Summer School Institute, and has coordinated the implementation of the Morningside Model at Riverside Indian School, an off-reservation boarding school in Anadarko, Oklahoma operating under the auspices of the Bureau of Indian Affairs. She has also authored and coauthored training materials for Morningside Teachers Academy. In her current role as executive assistant to the president of Central Washington University, she consults with Morningside Academy through a contract between Morningside and CWU.

PREFACE

This is a book about the remarkable student outcomes that teachers and schools can achieve by basing classroom practices upon scientific research in psychology and education. It is a book primarily for educators and other school professionals, and parents of school-aged children. Applied scientists, educational researchers, and educational psychologists may also find the book helpful in making sense of a vast scientific literature on how children learn, as well as indicating areas of educational practice that need further research. As such, the book is written more in the style one encounters in *The Atlantic Monthly*. It is not a book written for rigorous experimental scientists, although they may also find it helpful in delineating basic research questions in human learning. As such, the book is not written in research report style, with lots of last names and dates throughout. However, readers can easily trace the research trails by consulting the references we do cite.

Twenty-four years ago, Dr. Kent Johnson founded Morningside Academy in Seattle, Washington to provide scientifically-based academic and social programs for children and youth, and to prepare teachers and other school personnel. Since that time, Morningside has grown to be a complex corporation with three distinct programs serving each of the original goals. First, Morningside Academy is a school, operating during the school year and in summer. Second, Morningside Teachers' Academy participates in formal external partnerships with schools and agencies throughout the United States and Canada. It also offers a summer institute for teachers, graduate students, and other professionals. Morningside's programs are continually evolving to better prepare students for successful schooling and citizenry. Third,

3

Morningside Press publishes several key instructional programs responsible for student achievement in reading, writing, and mathematics. This book describes these programs and provides an update of a previous article and chapter (Johnson & Layng, 1992, 1994). It also expands on the program description and results that are reported in a recent chapter (Johnson & Street, in press).

The Morningside Model of Generative Instruction lies at the heart of this entire enterprise. The Model builds on five separate but overlapping streams of research: generativity and contingency adduction; content analysis, instructional design, and implementation; program placement and modification based on continuous measurement; classroom organization and management; and critical thinking, reasoning, and self-regulated decision-making. The 1992 article and 1994 chapter by Johnson and Layng credit the work of numerous behavior analysts and educators whose contributions are reflected in the model, only a few of which will be repeated here. In the chapters that follow, you will read about recent program developments and refinements in the Morningside Model of Generative Instruction; extensions of the model to more complex learning and real-world application; expanded coverage of the protocols that are used to assess and place students, and current data supporting its dissemination. The book is not a "how-to" manual for implementation but a more general description of our system. It is meant to stimulate interest and show what is possible when one lets scientific research be their guide. We hope the reader who wishes more education and training in our system will contact us.

Morningside Academy is a laboratory school in which curricular, management, and instructional elements are combined and recombined until a particular combination produces anticipated student gains on specified outcomes. Continuous formative assessment allows us to track the effectiveness of these curricular and instructional packages, and their effectiveness with many students in many classrooms gives us confidence that the combination is responsible for the outcome. We look for evidence that students' previous learning trajectories are replaced by speedier acquisition and more predictable application of new skills. However, what we do is not bench science. Specific elements of our combined procedures may or may not contribute to the overall outcome. Our methods of continuous formative measurement and pre- to post-test gains on summative measures, when viewed across students and classrooms and when compared to these students' past growth rates, convince us that our curricular and instructional packages are responsible for growth. But we, ourselves, don't employ elegant experimental designs in which all extraneous variables are controlled. Instead, we apply a variety of techniques that have shown promise in other settings, more to the end of producing promised outcomes. When students are not acquiring skills at a rate we've come to expect, we may change more than one thing at a time to achieve these anticipated improvement levels. We do, however, have ample opportunity to identify important research questions that we pass along to those who are prepared to employ empirical research designs to test them. In Chapter 12, we propose some of these questions in hopes that our colleagues will put them to rigorous tests.

We are indebted to Drs. T.V. Joe Layng, Warren Street, and Phil Chase for their thoughtful comments and editorial assistance during the development of this book. We also are indebted to the many teachers at Morningside and at partner schools and agencies whose feedback and insights have strengthened the Morningside Model and to the students whose learning has been the most important feedback of all. If, after reading this account, you'd like to know more about the work we do at Morningside Academy or to see the full array of materials that are available through Morningside Press, visit us online at http://www.morningsideacademy.org.

CHAPTER 1
ABOUT MORNINGSIDE

Morningside Academy

Current Work

Morningside Academy is a school that provides an opportunity for elementary and middle school students to catch up and get ahead. Most of its students performed poorly in their previous schools. Entering students typically score in the first and second quartiles on standardized achievement tests in reading, language, and mathematics. Some have diagnosed learning disabilities (LD); others are labeled as having attention deficit disorder (ADD) or attention deficit hyperactivity disorder (ADHD). Some lag behind their peer group for no "diagnosed" reason. Students' IQs range from low average to well above average. Less than two percent of our students are developmentally disabled or autistic. A small percentage of students have poor social relations with family members and friends, but most do not.

Morningside Academy's elementary school students typically enroll for one to three years to catch up to grade level. Many middle school students enroll for all of middle school. Morningside Academy offers a money-back guarantee for progressing two years in one in the skill of greatest deficit. Summed across its 23 years, Morningside Academy has returned less than one percent of school-year tuition.

Many models of education for children with mild learning disabilities and ADHD focus upon teaching children to employ compensatory strategies to sidestep their "disabilities." Morningside addresses the deficiencies of these children by directly teaching behavioral repertoires to build (a) basic academic skills, such as reading, writing, and mathematics; (b) learning skills, such as goal setting, listening,

7

noticing, reasoning, thinking, studying, and organizing; and (c) performance skills; that is, performing tasks in a timely, accurate, and organized manner without disrupting others or causing oneself undue grief. Morningside's program focuses upon these key academic, learning, and performance skills, and its accommodations for disabilities increase the intensity and explicitness of instruction.

The academic program focuses upon the three main foundation skills—reading, writing, and mathematics—including the language, facts, skills, concepts, principles, problem solving, and organizational components that comprise them. Literature, social studies, and science are the grist for teaching these foundations. Each student participates in extensive entry assessments of academic, learning, and performance skills. Students with similar needs and goals are grouped together for instruction. Groupings change repeatedly throughout the day as students move from reading to writing to mathematics. Groupings also change continuously throughout the school year as students make more or less progress than students in their current group.

The comprehensive reading program includes basic prerequisites such as print awareness, phonemic awareness through auditory blending and segmenting, and the alphabetic principle. Basic foundations in decoding are emphasized, including sound-symbol correspondence, textual blending and segmenting strategies, and reading fluency. Comprehension is a major focus. Students learn background information and vocabulary related to reading selections, which are organized according to universal life themes and research themes to provide solid springboards for later inquiry and research. Both basal reading programs and authentic literature are incorporated. Students also learn over 20 key comprehension skills such as recalling text in sequence, comparing and contrasting, and making inferences. Students learn to "read strategically" by asking questions, making connections with what they already know, making and confirming predictions, applying the comprehension skills they have learned, and so forth. They learn strategies for organizing and communicating their ongoing thoughts during discussion.

The comprehensive writing program includes mastery of rubrics for many different genres, including various descriptive, narrative, explanatory, and persuasive writing styles (Archer, 2002). Students master key component skills in handwriting, keyboarding, word processing, transcription, dictation, spelling, grammar, and mechanics; as well as organizational strategies such as selecting a topic, brainstorming details, and logically sequencing details, sentences, paragraphs, essays, and reports (Linden & Whimbey, 1990).

The comprehensive mathematics program includes mastery of counting and the numerical system, including such fundamentals as reading numbers, writing numbers, math facts, identifying place value, solving simple equations, factoring, and giving multiples of a number. Students also master calculation and other arithmetic skills and concepts, an area of mathematics education that often de-emphasized these days. Our curriculum balances computation and problem solving instruction. We teach students quantitative thinking, reasoning, and problem solving procedures that they apply along with their fluent arithmetic skills to solve real-world quantitative problems.

Morningside Academy's teachers coach students to perform their best. Teachers coach performance with clearly defined rules and expectations for performance and productivity, explicit modeling of high performance skills, and moment-to-moment monitoring and feedback. Students carry a daily report card throughout the day. Points are earned and recorded for meeting specific academic, learning skills, and citizenship aims that the teacher specifies before each class period. Students share their report cards with their families each day. Many students earn home-based rewards such as extra television, computer access, or telephone time for meeting their aims. In addition, classroom wall charts display the points that each student earns.

In the middle school, students also learn how to study and perform successfully in content classes in the social and natural sciences and the humanities. We are gradually adding content area subjects to our program, including world history, civics, general science, geography and culture, and human relations and communication. Each program will explicitly teach everything from textbook reading and studying and lecture note taking and studying to participation in class discussions, test taking, and essay and report writing. Morningside Academy's middle school program also includes after-school leisure activities in music, fine arts, theatre, sports, yoga, dance, and the martial arts.

Morningside Academy offers a 5-week summer school program that provides morning and afternoon programs in reading, language, writing, and mathematics. Some of our students attend school year round, focusing on their skill of greatest deficit. Many other students who do not have learning or attention problems and who are not behind in school attend Morningside to sharpen their basic skills and develop the necessary foundations for becoming high performers in school. Students typically gain a grade level in the skill area they study. The summer school program offers a money-back guarantee for progressing 1 year in the skill of greatest deficit. Summed over 23 years, Morningside Academy has returned less than two percent of summer school tuition.

The popularity of Morningside Academy's summer school program with children and youth who are at or above grade level attests to the dearth of good instruction in foundations skills in typical public and private schools. All students can benefit from part or all of Morningside's programs. The difference between upper and lower percentile students is the amount of time they need to spend in the Morningside programs. In fact, part of every school day at Skinner, a school for gifted children in Chicago, is devoted to Morningside's reading and math fluency programs.

Future Directions

In the course of learning fundamental reading, reasoning, mathematics, and writing skills, students already work together in pairs, talk aloud with each other to solve problems and understand text, and monitor their own progress. We make our techniques very transparent so students develop their own expertise about how we teach and how they learn. Visitors to Morningside Academy are often surprised that our older students can describe Morningside's teaching technologies just about as well as their teachers.

Now, we are turning our attention to teaching students how to apply their academic and learning skills to identify their own curiosities and areas of interest and work with other students to define collective research projects. In this effort, we are teaching the inquiry, research, and cooperative learning skills necessary for project-based learning.[2] We are also pursuing citizenship goals. We are also

---

[2] In project-based learning, students begin with a problem or topic that peaks their interest, apply existing knowledge and skills to it, seek additional information as needed, and ultimately develop an interesting or creative solution to the problem or an in-depth presentation of the topic. Depending on the teacher's philosophy and style, project-based learning may be directive or not. Students may nor may not be instructed in and have an opportunity to practice basic or fundamental skills in the context of their projects. Morningside adopts a bottom-up approach, ensuring that fundamental skills are firm, before engaging students in project-based

encouraging students to identify problems of concern to everyday living, inform themselves about the issues, and inquire and research together. We want our students to take control of their own learning and to apply the skills they've already learned to self-initiated common goals. These kinds of projects also provide an opportunity for students to perfect essential human relations skills.

As students collaborate, they will apply a scientific method of inquiry to real-world areas of interest. They will define research goals and possible courses of action to achieve them. They will learn observation and other data gathering methods. They will learn a recursive cycle in which they actively question their process, develop ideas or conjectures, revise ideas, and embark upon new avenues of research and exploration as they proceed. They will also learn methods of analyzing data and making generalizations.

As students research their problems and interests, they will make contact with books, periodicals, video, lectures, the Internet, libraries, and community workplaces and events. Students will also learn communication and outreach skills. They will invite community members to their forums, make multi-media presentations, develop oratory style, and write pamphlets, handouts, and reports. The inquiry, research, collaborative learning, and presentation skills that the students will learn from completing projects provide a framework for life-long learning, stemming from their own needs and interests into the systematized knowledge of the adult world.

---

learning. We discuss this approach and the underlying philosophy in more detail in Chapter 5.

Morningside Teachers' Academy

Many individual teachers, graduate students, parents, and professionals have learned of our successes and have requested our help to bring Morningside's programs to their children and schools.

External Partnerships

Morningside Teachers' Academy helps others implement its programs through formal external partnerships with public and private schools and agencies. Our collaboration with each school is extensive, usually lasting from three to five years. Four main goals of these external partnerships are (1) to help all students achieve grade level performance, (2) to teach their faculty assessment, teaching, and learning strategies that will serve them throughout their teaching career in all areas of the curriculum, (3) to teach their principals how to become instructional leaders and support their faculty's teaching efforts, and (4) to help develop implementation, teacher education, and internal coaching systems to maintain our efforts after we exit.

Teachers learn to assess and place their own students in our foundations programs. We provide 40–60 hours of workshops and 30–50 days of individualized, in-classroom coaching per school year. During coaching we partner with the teacher as she teaches, providing encouragement, demonstrating effective strategies, and guiding the teacher's practice of the methods she has learned in our workshops. Research on teacher education makes clear the power and importance of coaching teachers in their own classrooms. Bennett (1987) reports that, without follow-up in-classroom coaching, teachers implement less than 10% of what they learn in courses and workshops. To counter this problem,

Morningside provides more basic coaching for new teachers and consults frequently with teachers, specialty staff, and the principal. Morningside maintains frequent contact with school district personnel as well, focusing upon problem solving, program expansion, and self–maintenance, including train-the-trainer models that are suited to a school district's ongoing relationship with its schools. As of this writing, 86 schools and agencies throughout the United States and Canada have contracted for partnerships since 1991.

Summer School Institute (SSI)

Morningside Teachers' Academy also offers a four–week intensive summer institute for individual teachers, graduate students, parents, and other professionals who want to learn our programs. Participants can earn graduate credits. Over 300 hundred professionals have attended SSI since its inception in 1991. Individuals may also contract for school year internships and sabbaticals and experience a customized institute.

Morningside Press

Morningside Academy applies Dr. Susan Markle's (1990) instructional design principles to design its own instruction and fluency materials in reading, writing, mathematics, test preparation, classroom management, and academic assessment. Most are supplementary practice materials to be used in conjunction with other commercially available materials. For example, we have developed extensive fluency practice materials to accompany Dr. Anita Archer's *REWARDS* and *REWARDS Plus*, Siegfried Engelmann's *Expressive Writing*, and Dr. Arthur Whimbey's *Keys to Quick Writing Skills*. Some are stand-alone fluency practice materials that may accompany any other core academic program, such as Morningside Math Facts. A few are stand-alone core programs, such as *Morningside Addition and Subtraction Problem Solving*. Our *Daily Report Card* program will be available for purchase this year, as well as our *Precision Program Placement* system (see Table 1 in a later section of this chapter for a more complete list of programs).

Morningside Technology Transfer

Each Morningside program is competency and mastery-based, with a set of procedures and expected outcomes for both learners and teachers. Morningside takes an applied science approach to teaching the competencies to mastery. In the Morningside system, research-based components of curriculum and instruction are combined into a generic model of teaching and learning. The science of human learning informs the generic model, just as engineering is informed by its parent-science, physics. We will describe the generic model, The Morningside Model of Generative Instruction, later in the book. In this section we will describe the origins of the curriculum and instruction components that we draw upon.

In a continuing expansion of best practices, Morningside's leadership:

- Scours the psychology and education literature, the academic and educational communities, and the education marketplace, seeking effective research–based materials, learner-verified methods, and tools to use during instruction, practice, assessment, and measurement of performance.
- Selects certain research-based curricula and instructional methods that target areas of current

practice that could be improved to user-test at the Academy.

- Adapts these materials, methods, and tools to Morningside's behavioral framework for teaching.
- User-tests the curricula, methods, and tools at the Academy and collects data on student and teacher performance.
- Develops workshops to teach others how to implement programs that demonstrate better results than current practices
- User-tests the workshops and program offsite, with a veteran external partner school.
- Revises the workshops and makes further adaptations to the program.
- Continuously assesses outcome data for students until gains that meet specified criteria are consistently achieved (see Chapter 11 for student outcome data).
- Designates the program a technology. By technology, we mean that it is replicable: a program that can be specified, and taught to others.
- Transfers the technologies by marketing them to others as part of the "Morningside Model of Generative Instruction."

These procedures make Morningside Academy a laboratory school in the spirit of Dr. John Dewey's schools in Chicago and New York at the beginning of the twentieth century (Dewey, 1900, 1902). Dr. Carl Binder (1988) has described the laboratory nature of Morningside's work in more depth.

Examples of Verified Technologies for Transfer

In the last decade, in addition to the materials we publish through Morningside Press, a host of programs (see Table 1)[3] have been user-tested and adapted to meet the criteria for a Morningside technology.

Table 1. Programs that Morningside has User-Tested and Adapted

Reading	*Headsprout Reading* (http://www.headsprout.com)
	Read Well (Sopris West)
	Scott Foresman Reading 2002
	Teach Your Children to Read Well (http://www.teachyourchildrenwell.com)
	Open Court (SRA/McGraw Hill)
	Haughton's Phonemic Awareness Series (Haughton Learning Center)
	Basic Elements (Morningside)
	REWARDS (Sopris West)
	Reading Mastery (SRA/McGraw-Hill)
	The Power of Retelling (McGraw-Hill/The Wright Group)
	Mastering Reading Through Reasoning (Innovative Sciences, Inc.)
	Analytical Reading and Reasoning (Innovative Sciences, Inc.)
Mathematics	*Saxon Math* (Saxon Publishers)
	Morningside Mathematics Tools (Morningside Press)
	Beyond Problem Solving & Comprehension (Lawrence Erlbaum, Inc.)

continued...

[3]Readers are invited to submit other instructional programs and materials to Morningside for review.

Writing	*Expressive Writing* (SRA/McGraw-Hill) *An Instructional Approach to Teaching Composition* (Anita Archer, developmental draft, 2002) *Keys to Quick Writing Skills* (EBSCO Curriculum Materials) + *Keys To Quick Writing Fluency* (Morningside Press) *Grammar for Writing and Reading Skills* (BGF Inc.)
Thinking and Reasoning	*Problem Solving and Comprehension* (Lawrence Erlbaum, Inc.), *Fluent Thinking Skills* (Robbins, Layng & Jackson, developmental draft, 1996), *Thinking Through Math Word Problems* (Lawrence Erlbaum, Inc.) *TAPS For Teachers* (Robbins, draft, 1996).

Each Morningside program is a synthesis of several technologies of teaching, learning, assessment, measurement, classroom implementation, and management that has proved effective in data-based research studies. The ingredients for any particular mix may include a particular *curriculum* (that is, learning objectives; print or software materials; objects, devices, or tools) that has been developed, particular *instruction*—teaching or practice methods—that could be used with a curriculum, or a pre-existing *program*—a combination of curriculum and instruction. We have added teaching methods, including direct instruction, delayed prompting, and fluency-building, to curricular and basal series that are in common use in public and private school classrooms. In reading, for example, we have combined Morningside technologies with SRA/McGraw Hill's *Open Court 2002*, Holt, Rinehart, and Winston's *Elements of Literature,* and Scott Foresman's *Reading 2002.*

Because classrooms may differ in format and development within a given school or program, one or more curricula, instructional methods, or programs may be combined as a recommended "technology package" for a particular grade level or student need. This interplay among content analysis (see Chapter 3), assessment (see Chapter 4), instructional design (See Chapter 5), and site-specific characteristics (see Chapter 10) makes the Morningside Model both diagnostic and prescriptive, and the specific mix of technologies that is selected for use in any given classroom is customized based upon an elaborate assessment of learners' and teachers' needs and skills.

CHAPTER 2
THE MORNINGSIDE MODEL OF
GENERATIVE INSTRUCTION:
PHILOSOPHICAL UNDERPINNINGS

In their 1992 article in the *American Psychologist,* Johnson and Layng described the Morningside Model of Generative Instruction. The Morningside Model prescribes a stepwise progression through an instructional sequence from entry to true mastery of an objective and aligns classroom practices with each step in the progression. Instruction has three phases: acquisition or establishment, practice for fluency, and application. True mastery is defined as performance that is accurate, speedy, durable, smooth, and useful. Although the model has been refined, much of what was written in that seminal article continues to characterize the model today.

Underpinning the model is the selectionist approach to understanding human behavior advocated by psychologist Dr. B.F. Skinner and the progressive philosopher Dr. John Dewey. B.F. Skinner first advocated a selectionist approach to understanding human behavior in 1969 in *Contingencies of Reinforcement: A Theoretical Analysis.* Compared to a structuralist approach, which emphasizes form and process, the selectionist approach emphasizes the function of particular behaviors in meeting environmental contingencies. Skinner draws a parallel between the emergence of complex behavioral repertoires and the emergence of more complex and variably functional forms in evolutionary biology. The environment selects simple forms, and a more complex entity gradually emerges. In the case of human behavior, reinforcement or success selects the element. In evolutionary biology, natural section is responsible. The Morningside Model represents a selectionist approach to understanding complex human behavior and designing instructional protocols. The program

20

builds complex intellectual skills from combinations of elements. In addition, the model is, itself, evolutionary. It responds to emerging evidence, refining some practices and discarding others that are ineffective in meeting important educational contingencies.

John Dewey's American pragmatism and philosophy of education (1900, 1902, 1916, 1938) describes the kind of selectionist process that occurs during the advanced segments of the Morningside continuum of curriculum and instruction. Dewey emphasizes natural influences over learning, taken from the student's current activity, goals, and values systems. It is in these natural contexts that students select subject matter to learn, rather than learning subject matter solely in arbitrary pre-packaged courses such as Earth Science and Modern British Literature. Likewise, Dewey emphasizes student-initiated research, as the interest or need-to-know arises for the student, rather than teacher-initiated research topics. For Dewey, this selection process is naturalistic and evolving, leading different learners down different functional paths in the real world. Morningside's program begins with basic elements and tools and builds repertoires that make possible the kind of naturally reinforced learning that is characteristic of project-based learning and Dewey's progressive education.

As Dr. Skinner himself has declared, the model of education he describes in *Walden II* (1948) derives directly from John Dewey's work (Evans, 1968). In the 1950s and 1960s Skinner changed his viewpoint and emphasized the need for a more technical approach to education, a technology of teaching (1968; see also Barrett, 2003). The Morningside Model of Generative Instruction sees a continuum that begins with a more technological approach, with the teacher fully in charge of seeding the repertoires of the naïve learner with generalized imitative "how to" repertoires of reading, reasoning, writing, mathematics, learning, studying, problem solving, and completing projects in a transmission of culture. Morningside's curriculum ladders specify over 400 instructional objectives related to these "how to" repertoires. When students master these foundations, Morningside advocates switching to a more Deweyian approach in which students apply their foundations in a personal and naturally reinforcing manner. Thus the Morningside Model maps a continuum from teacher-driven instruction to student-centered application.

Relation of Skinner's and Dewey's Philosophies to Instructivist and Constructivist Practices

Two derivatives of the philosophic beliefs of Skinner and Dewey are instructivism and constructivism, although both instructivism and constructivism sometimes diverge considerably from the writings of these two intellectual giants. Instructivism and constructivism are often presented as diametrically opposed beliefs about the nature of knowledge and of knowing; however, Morningside has benefited from both perspectives, and Morningside technologies integrate the best features of each.

Instructivism refers to a set of educational practices consistent with the philosophy and findings of behavioral psychologists. Instructivism is an approach to education that places the teacher in charge of instruction and learning. Their credo is if the student isn't learning, the teacher isn't teaching. Instructivism favors thorough content analysis, identification of tool and component skills, carefully crafted educational sequences that build elemental knowledge into complex wholes, and an emphasis on building fluency of component skills as a way to encourage the emergence of untaught behaviors (see, for example, Finn & Ravitch, 1996; Kozloff,

Lanunziata, Cowardin, & Bessellieu, 2001). Instructivism harkens to Skinner who declared, "The principal function of education is to transmit the culture—to enable new members of a group to profit from what others have already learned. It follows that the principal task of the student is to learn what others already know" (Skinner, 1978, p. 149). Students receive explicit instruction in the conventions and codes of the culture, for example, the symbolic code for translating oral language into written language or for describing the numeric properties of nature. Instructivists accept that these contrived symbolic systems stand for natural processes or describe natural objects and events, but do not view the symbolic systems themselves as "natural" or discoverable. Instructivism is a molecular approach to educational practice.

A distant cousin of Dewey's philosophy is constructivism. Constructivism refers to a set of educational practices consistent with the philosophy and findings of developmental psychologists and some cognitive psychologists. In fact, while constructivists lay claim to Deweyian philosophy, the approach is as often credited to Piaget (1972) and Vygotsky (1978, 1986). Constructivism is an approach that favors student exploration of content and processes in authentic contexts. Students are encouraged to construct their own knowledge by testing ideas and integrating new knowledge with pre-existing intellectual constructs. The approach favors natural ontogenesis of learning consistent with the learner's optimal developmental trajectory. Knowledge is thought to be temporary, developmental, subjective, internally constructed, and socially and culturally mediated. Learners are thought to construct knowledge through cooperative social activity, discourse, and debate (see, for example, Packer & Goicoechea, 2000; Phillips, 1995, 1997; Richardson, 1997; Von Glaserfeld, 1997). Constructivism is a molar approach to educational practice.

Although there are many features that Dewey's pragmatism and constructivism share, Dewey's laboratory school was really as much instructivistic as constructivistic. While the learner's interests and "need-to-knows" drive a Deweyian classroom, the teacher shares responsibility for using and extending those interests and "need-to-knows" relevant to a curriculum agenda. Dewey's philosophy is closer to Skinner's *Walden II* position, emphasizing the need for the consequences of learning to be naturally reinforcing to the learner. In fact, the core basis of American pragmatism is the notion that truth or utility of an action or belief lays in its consequences or outcomes. The "consequences" aspects of Dewey's pragmatism are not highlighted in constructivism, nor is the reality-base of Dewey's curriculum given much prominence in the approach. In fact, a recent history of psychology brands Dewey the "philosophical behaviorist" of the 1920s (Bringmann, Luck, Miller, & Early, 1997).

There is wide latitude in the beliefs represented by people in the instructivistic and constructivistic camps; still, some summary statements about the positions of each group are possible. Very simply put, instructivists believe that formal knowledge is an imperfect and evolving verbal representation of a physical reality, whereas constructivists believe that formal knowledge is socially and individually constructed and does not necessarily represent a physical reality. Instructivists believe that important economies can be realized when instructional programs organize and synthesize current thinking about the natural world and communicate their findings in an orderly way to learners. Constructivists believe that students should learn about the world through direct experience with it. Constrained, scripted lessons are abandoned in favor of exploration in which learners are free to make choices and take matters into their own hands.

Constructivists have contended that instructivists serve political conservatism, discourage thoughtful reflection on conventional thinking and formal knowledge, maintain the status quo, and transmit a myopic view of the world. Instructivists, on the other hand, have reasoned that constructivists provide no foundation upon which the learner can explore the world and leave it to the learner to discover arbitrary codes that have no basis in the natural world. Constructivist practices either implicitly or explicitly assume that all learners are equally prepared to benefit from exploration. Instructivists believe the assumption is dangerously naïve, one that widens rather than lessens the gap between the powerful and the disenfranchised. (Readers interested in knowing more may enjoy two particularly thoughtful articles. First, well-known cognitive psychologists Drs. John Anderson, Lynn Reder, and Herb Simon (1996) examine some of the most common constructivist's criticism of instructivist practices. Second, reading expert Dr. Michael Pressley and his colleague reexamine their own thinking about constructivism and instruction (Pressley & Harris, 1997).

As we will see later in this book, the Morningside Model of Generative Instruction blends these two ways of thinking about teaching and learning, favoring instructivist practices to build a foundation for thinking and reflection and favoring a Deweyian approach to natural reinforcement that makes some use of constructivist practices to build reflective, thoughtful learners who are socially conscious and engaged with the world around them.

CHAPTER 3
CURRICULUM AND ITS SEQUENCE

Generativity and Contingency Adduction

The Morningside Model is a model of generative instruction. It hinges on the belief that complex behavioral repertoires emerge without explicit instruction when well-selected component repertoires are appropriately sequenced, carefully instructed, and well-rehearsed.

The earliest influence on the model came from Dr. Charles Ferster, whose 1965 paper "Verbal Behavior As Magic" asserted that new learning and novel behavior is a result of a rearrangement of existing repertoires. Each new, more complex behavior emerges in an evolution from previous learnings. At least two terms have recently been applied to these naturally occurring phenomena: generativity and contingency adduction.

Dr. Robert Epstein, a student of B.F. Skinner, used the term generativity to describe a phenomenon witnessed in a series of animal laboratory experiments that were intended to provide a behavioral interpretation of insight (Epstein, 1991; Epstein, Kirshnit, Lanza, & Rubin, 1984). They found that pigeons who were taught to push a small box around an experimental chamber, to step on the box, and to peck at an object—all in separate training sessions—would solve the problem of pecking at the object when it was out of reach. When presented with the problem, birds would demonstrate a series of maneuvers often credited to insight. In remarkably similar behavior patterns, birds would observe the experimental chamber, move the box under the banana, step on the box, and peck the banana. Only birds that received instruction in all three of the component skills successfully solved the problem. Epstein referred to this phenomenon as generativity, which he defined as the "spontaneous" (unprompted, not arranged) interconnection of existing repertoires to solve a problem. He later expanded this work to show the emergence of novel behaviors in humans.

Drs. Paul Andronis, Joe Layng, and Israel Goldiamond (1997) applied the term contingency adduction to a related phenomenon. In their account, new contingencies or performance requirements may recruit performances learned under other contingencies. That is, when circumstances are right, the learner engages in behavior in a new setting that has earned reinforcement in a previously encountered situation. The performance is reinforced in that new setting often by a different class or type of reinforcement. The moment of reinforcement marks the moment of contingency adduction. They used the term "contingency adduction" rather than "adduction" to emphasize that the learner does not adduce the performance, the new contingency does. The new contingency shares common features with the original contingencies that produced the performance. Contingencies can adduce multiple or combined patterns. The term adduction is applied in its definitional sense of "drawing from." In this book we will use the term contingency adduction as an umbrella term for all generative processes and the occurrence of novel behavior.[4]

Johnson and Layng (1992) provided evidence of a simple contingency-adduction of fractions problem solving

---

[4] The concept of contingency adduction can be used to describe all of the phenomena related to the occurrence of novel behavior, including stimulus and response generalization, extension, concept formation, recombinations and interconnections of repertoires, and stimulus class formations and equivalence (Joe Layng, personal communication, 1994; Paul Andronis, personal communication, 1994). Although it is not as well researched empirically as some of the individual phenomena we mention here, it promises to be the most conceptually encompassing and least restrictive of the generative process terms.

performance, after students were instructed in whole number problem solving and fractions computation. Students demonstrated fractions problem solving before the teacher presented the lesson, but only after instruction and practice in key component repertoires that recombine in fractions problem solving. As Morningside teachers move through the curriculum sequence, they routinely present opportunities for learners to demonstrate recombinative skills before instructing them. They may ask simple questions such as "Can you do this problem now?" or they may provide a demonstration of more complex recombinations and give students the opportunity to imitate them. Students who can demonstrate the new skill with little or no instruction are moved ahead in the curriculum. Drs. Joe Layng, Janet Twyman, and Greg Stikeleather have also demonstrated contingency adduction with preschoolers in a beginning reading program (Layng, Twyman, & Stikeleather, 2004).

Dr. Galen Alessi's pivotal paper in 1987 discussed the implications of generativity for the design and power of instruction. He reasoned that many curricular strands[5] have an infinite set of relationships, each of which cannot be taught directly. Instead, children learn to respond to a general case; they learn a general pattern of responding that produces effective responding to many untrained relations. The elegance of an instructional program depends on the programmer's ability to detect and teach some minimal response or

---

[5] Curriculum strands are subdivisions of knowledge and skills within a larger content area. They emerge from content analyses and often are described in a scope and sequence chart that guides the order of introduction of strands and of skills within the strands. For example, within reading, the first level of analysis reveals at least seven different dimensions: phonological coding, decoding, reading fluency and prosity, vocabulary, remembering what has been read, comprehension skills, and strategic application of comprehension skills.

generative set which can combine and recombine into the universal set of all possible relationships. One is looking, very simply, for the exponential value of key instructional events, in which behaviors that emerge are in a power relation to the elements that are taught. It is on this basis that many educators believe that instruction in decoding produces greater power than instruction in sight-reading or contextual cueing. Successful sight reading instruction and practice will reliably create the performance of reading the sight words as they arise in text in the future, but no other reading performance is guaranteed. Successful phonics and word attack instruction, on the other hand, will reliably produce recombinative reading behavior, guaranteeing successful reading of thousands of words beyond those taught in original instruction. Alessi points out that by blending various of the 40 or so letter-sound combinations in the English language, a child can read any of nearly 500,000 words, yielding an average "generative or multiplicative power of over 10,000. That is, the child would be able to decode on average 10,000 novel words for every discrete sound-symbol element taught. . . .Teaching reading of English by sight words (cf. rote memory) is a nongenerative alternative. . ." (Alessi, 1987, p. 18).[6] Clearly, some curricular

---

[6] This is not to say that children cannot induce decoding rules from examples. From a behavioral approach, decoding is a rule-governed, deductive method for teaching aspects of reading. In the 1960s, Dr. James Evans developed deductive teaching methods which he called the *RulEg* approach (Evans, Homme, & Glaser, 1962). Sight reading, on the other hand, is a contingency-shaped, inductive method of teaching reading. (Evans developed *EgRul methods for inductive teaching*.) While Alessi's argument that the expository method is more efficient has been supported by decades of research on the topic, there is some evidence that the discovery approach is more likely to create response variation that is critical to respond to new situations. Because Morningside focuses on learners who are already behind their same-age peers in acquiring reading skills, the more efficient, deductive method is employed, and students learn critical

strands lend themselves more easily to teaching the general case than others. As Alessi notes, there is considerably more generative potential in designing instruction in the metric system of measurement than the English system of measurement. Still, the point is clear. Instructional programs that detect and instruct a minimal response set are considerably more efficient and more powerful than programs that attempt to teach every stimulus–response relation.

Although the phenomenon of contingency adduction or generativity is naturally-occurring, the arrangement of events to maximize its occurrence is not. The specific sequences of skills and the focus upon teaching minimum response repertoires and establishing the general case make Morningside programs generative in design. Morningside carefully constructs instructional programs so that learners experience contingency adduction on a regular basis. Instructional programs are built on a logical and empirical analysis of the knowledge, skills, and relationships in a field of study. Skills are introduced in an order that makes it most likely that previously learned skills will be recruited to meet new performance requirements. Many of Siegfried Engelmann's Direct Instruction programs are also built in this way; it is no surprise that Morningside includes the best of those on its recommended program list. Morningside adds an extra level of potency by using "fluency building" practice procedures. The goal of fluency building is to build hardy academic behaviors—behaviors that weather periods of no practice, occur with short latencies, are impervious to distraction, and are easily accessible in new situations. More on this later.

---

thinking repertoires to form a bridge between existing skills and the requirements of novel situations. Still, there are some interesting empirical questions to be pursued here (see Chapter 12).

In his book *Guns, Germs, and Steel*, Jared Diamond (1997) writes of the explosion of technology that began in the 19th century and continues at an astonishing pace. He says, "Because technology begets more technology, the importance of an invention's diffusion potentially exceeds the importance of the original invention. Technology's history exemplifies what is termed an autocatalytic process: that is, one that speeds up at a rate that increases with time, because the process catalyzes itself" (p. 258).

There is a parallel at Morningside, where instructional designers and teachers make decisions about content and instructional processes to ensure that learning will beget more learning—that learning will catalyze itself. The Morningside model is intentional in its attempt to achieve an explosion of learning. As contingency adduction accelerates, students become successful at the kind of naturally occurring learning that John Dewey advocates.

A System of Instruction

Morningside adopts a systematic and scientific approach to instruction that builds on a system of instruction first outlined by Drs. Susan Markle and Philip Tiemann (1967) at the University of Illinois at Chicago. Instructional protocols are developed according to a set of principles, and programs are tested on naïve learners to ensure they produce intended results.

Our adaptation of Markle and Tiemann's system of instruction is presented in Figure 1. It includes six components. First, designers begin with clearly stated goals and *objectives* that the learner is expected to achieve.

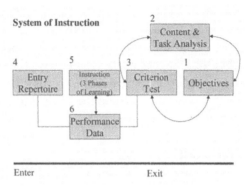

Figure 1. Markle and Tiemann's system of instruction (adapted from Markle & Tiemann, 1967).

Second, based on the intended outcomes, *content and task analyses* are conducted for the purpose of identifying curricular tasks on which mastery of terminal objectives hinges. Third, designers also construct *criterion tests* that fairly represent the stated outcomes and that have a measure of social validity. These criterion tests are designed before instruction is designed and implemented to assure that the subsequent instructional design is directly based upon expected posttest performance and that post-testing is not based upon incidentals that occur during the instructional process. Fourth, care is taken to specify the *entry repertoire* the learner must possess in order to be successful in the program. Additional entering behavior pretests are designed to guarantee that students have mastered all necessary prerequisites for upcoming instruction. Fifth, an *instructional sequence* is designed to establish the minimum set of instructional tasks through which the learner must proceed to achieve the pre-stated outcomes. Sixth, *performance data* are collected throughout instruction, and the program is adjusted as necessary, based upon these data. Performance data from naïve learners serves as evidence of the effectiveness of an instructional sequence or of the need for additional modifications. The sequence of topics in this book follows the sequence of elements in Markle and Tiemann's instructional system.

Markle and Tiemann's system of instruction either directly or indirectly underpins all modern-day explicit instructional approaches, including direct instruction broadly defined (see, for example, Dr. Barak Rosenshine's work at the University of Illinois. 1997), and Direct Instruction as more strictly defined by Siegfried Engelmann and his colleagues at the University of Oregon (see, for example, Engelmann & Carnine, 1982). The system can be applied to entire fields of study or to curricular strands within a field. For example, it can be applied to the whole of mathematics as a content field or it can be applied more narrowly to teaching an entire nation the metric system of measurement. Central to the approach are 1) reliance on thoroughgoing analysis of the content area that is the subject for instruction; 2) an understanding of what Robert Gagne (1965, 1970, 1977, 1985) and others have called types of learning, learning typologies, or learning outcomes that inform instructional protocols; 3) ordering of elements in the curriculum to ensure that learners progress through it seamlessly; 4) elegant instructional protocols that achieve outcomes with the minimum amount of instructional intervention; 5) field testing and fine-tuning of curricular assumptions and instructional programs at every turn.

Morningside likes this system because it, too, is an evolutionary system. Programs are evaluated on the basis of their ability to produce happy, competent learners who are naturally reinforced by progress. When they don't, they are changed. This is particularly important because of the lasting side effects of programs that produce failure. When instructional protocols are unsuccessful, they create a motivational problem that becomes harder and harder to solve.

Learners who experience continual failure simply begin to disengage from the set of tasks to which they attribute that failure (Turner, Midgley, Meyer, Gheen, Anderman, Kang, & Patrick, 2002). When learners describe themselves as math phobic, for example, it most often means that they no longer risk the failure that has been associated with previous efforts to master mathematics. However, learners and others often use such failures to draw conclusions about ability, rather than about the relative effectiveness of the curriculum. Thus, Morningside designers strive for a path through the curriculum that makes each successive task at least as easy to learn as the one that preceded it and a path that prevents failure or repairs the effects of historic failure.

Establishing Objectives and Analyzing Content

When Morningside designers develop an interest in a content area, they read research in the field, examine scope and sequence charts from a variety of curricular materials, and review existing instructional protocols. They draw from work within all philosophic camps and extend the reach of their investigation to authors that are not in mainstream publications.

The work of establishing instructional objectives and analyzing content is interdependent rather than linear because the content field is not transparent. The skills required to master the terminal goals are not readily apparent, and the optimal path through the content—one that inspires generativity and contingency adduction—is not always obvious. Casual knowledge of a subject field rarely yields the in-depth understanding that is needed to develop an elegant and parsimonious curriculum.

Typically, a general goal is established, and the instructional design team begins a dance between understanding the topic of study and setting explicit objectives that derive from it. Content analysis uncovers critical foundational skills that learners must master to meet terminal goals. For many learners, no amount of instruction on a higher-level objective will result in mastery if its component foundation skills are not shored up.

Content analysis at Morningside is of two primary types: content-dependent and content-independent.

Content-Dependent Analysis

Content-dependent analysis begins with an understanding of the knowledge and skills to be acquired, their linear and synergistic relations to each other, and the ways in which expertise in the subject field is socially validated. This understanding provides a basis from which to establish content hierarchies and instructional sequences. It also informs the designation of prerequisite skills on which content mastery is contingent.

As Morningside's content analysts become familiar with the overall contour of the content area, they identify major skill sets within it. Think of major skill sets as the socially validated goals of instruction within a content area. For example, reading is a multidimensional ability that includes several major skill sets that have been variously organized by experts in the field. Table 2 provides one organizational scheme.

The most complete content-dependent analyses cover the full range of real-world activities characteristic of the domain and analyze them into their most elementary units. Once major skills sets are identified, analysts attempt to discover the broad range of sub-skills and knowledge that make up these socially validated outcomes. Fine-grained task analyses reveal tool skills and component skills that constitute the authentic outcomes.

Table 2. An Organizational Framework for Reading (Johnson, 2001)

Tool Skills	Component Skills, Elements	Composite Skills, Compounds
Phonemic and Print Awareness	*Accessing Background Knowledge*	*Comprehension Strategies*
Phonological coding		Use existing
Orthographic coding	*Vocabulary Building*	knowledge to
Oral/print	Building the	make sense of
correspondence	lexicon (e.g.,	text
Print and book	power words)	Ask questions
conventions and	Determining	Answer
mechanics.	meaning from	questions
	text	Clarify meaning
Contextualized		Make
Language and Listening	*Comprehension Skills*	connections
Turn taking	Drawing	Predict
Syntax (word order)	conclusions	Confirm
Semantics/	Identifying author's	predictions
vocabulary	point of view	Summarize
Morphology	Identifying author's	Visualize
Tacting and manding	purpose	Use
Language of	Identifying cause	comprehension
instruction	and effect	skills in
Pretelling and	Classifying/	context
retelling—	categorizing	
nontextual	Comparing/	*Self-monitoring*
Thinking and problem	contrasting	*strategies*
solving	Distinguishing fact	Match reading
	from opinion	rate and
Decoding fluency	Distinguishing	strategies to
Single syllable	reality from	purpose
Multisyllable	fantasy	Monitoring for
	Retelling	consistent
		use of skills and
	Text Structure	strategies
	Fluency	Making
		appropriate
		decisions
		about when to
		re-read

Underlying knowledge and skills are organized to discover common foundational skills, common second-level skills, and so on. In essence, the analyst builds, from the various major skill sets, a series of overlapping pyramids that have common foundational building blocks and some common component skills. This work serves three purposes: it reveals a hierarchy of foundational skills which, when mastered, will aid in acquisition of a number of higher-level skills. It also reveals where particular skills should be inserted into the scope and sequence. Last, it clarifies when order of presentation of a skill in the instructional sequence is critical and when it is not. Fundamentally, Morningside programmers look for the minimal response or generative skill sets (Alessi, 1987) that will produce the optimal multiplicative power.

As the process is finalized, the content area, or some sub-set of it, is characterized as a set of **tool skills**, those minimal response sets which underpin virtually all other skills in the content area, a set of **component skills or elements**, the second level of building blocks that depend on one or more tool skills, and **compounds** or **composite repertoires**, higher level performances that socially validate the learner's mastery of the content area. The Morningside model assumes that compound repertoires are, in large part, generative; they derive from combinations and recombinations of component skills and emerge when skills that comprise them, along with integrative skills, are well-established. This content analysis process is critical to establishing a scope and sequence that results in seamless and relatively effortless learning. Tables 3 and 4 depict examples of tool, component skills, and compound repertoires for arithmetic and writing, respectively.

Table 3. Examples of Tools, Component Elements, and Compounds from Arithmetic

Tool Skills	Component Elements	Compounds, Composites
Saying numbers	Column addition	Solving addition and subtraction word problems, using whole numbers, fractions, and decimals
Reading numbers	Subtraction with regrouping	Solving multiplication & division word problems, using whole numbers, fractions, and decimals
Writing numbers	Long multiplication	Multi-step word problems
Identifying place value of digits	Long division	Applications in personal accounting
Math facts	Computation with fractions	Applications in budgeting
Rounding numbers	Computation with decimals	Applications in shopping

The designation of skills as tools, components, or compounds is relative to the entry repertoire and the terminal objective of an instructional program. A skill that is designated as a component skill in one instructional curriculum may become a tool skill in another. For example, learners who have mastered basic arithmetic, also known as basic numeracy, move on to other major skill sets within mathematics—geometry, algebra, trigonometry, the calculus, or statistics—where skills that had been designated as component skills now become tool skills for the new area. For example, facility with basic operations and ability to solve for an unknown in a simple equation, which may be component skills in basic arithmetic, become tool skills in the context of teaching algebra.

Table 4. Examples of Categories of Tools, Component Elements, and Compounds from Writing

Tool Skills	Components	Compounds
Transcription writing typing	Grammar & usage	Paragraphs written in a variety of genres, and styles within each genre
Dictation writing typing	Mechanics	Compositions and essays written in a variety of genres, and styles within each genre
Spelling	Sentence structure	

Content-Independent Analysis

In addition to content-dependent analyses, Morningside designers analyze content according to content-independent typologies. Two primary typologies form the basis of this work: learning channel analysis and learning outcomes analysis.

Learning Channels. Dr. Eric Haughton (1980) applied the term **learning channel** to a method of describing objectives on the basis of their stimulus and response characteristics. Stimulus characteristics, in this model, are defined in terms of the sensory organ through which the stimulus is experienced. Thus, a stimulus can be visual, auditory, tactile, olfactory, or gustatory. Translating these sensory experiences into everyday language, Haughton referred to them as see, hear, touch, smell, and taste. Later, he added "think" to reference stimuli that are not present in the external environment but rather reside in the history of the learner. Currently, the "think" channel is referred to as "free," that is, free of any clearly visible sensory input. Response characteristics were described on the basis of common movements, for example, say, write, point, and do. A stimulus–response pair is called a learning channel. Each learning objective, then, is preceded by a learning channel. For example, instruction to ensure that a learner "knows" his numbers in early arithmetic might include see/say numbers; see/write numbers; hear/say numbers; hear/write numbers; free/say numbers; and free/write numbers.

Learning channels may sound similar to learning modalities or learning styles, but the approach differs in several significant ways. Both specify stimulus and performance characteristics of a task and both explicitly assume that achieving mastery of content in one channel, modality, or style doesn't necessarily result in its mastery in another. They differ, however, in at least four ways. Proponents of learning styles tend to view ability or disability with respect to a specific sensory motor channel as a function of hard-wired individual differences, whereas proponents of learning channels assume that ability is a function of the learner's past teaching and learning history. Learning style proponents conduct general assessments using instruments that typically have low reliability. Learning channel proponents assess task-specific channel competence and diagnose tool skill and fluency deficits that need to be remedied to improve performance. Learning style proponents recommend teaching to the learner's channel strength. Learning channel proponents recommend teaching, within each curriculum strand, all channels that are required to use content effectively in authentic situations. Learning style advocates recommend that, should it be necessary to require performance in a weak modality, the learner should be taught an accommodation, for example, translating from a strong modality to a weak modality. Learning channel advocates establish baseline rates on weak channels and design interventions to systematically and directly improve performance. For example, if students usually perform at low frequencies whenever a task requires the auditory channel, a teacher will provide them with a regimen of auditory discrimination exercises across a variety of high-interest topics (e.g., strange animal or plant names, nonsense words), and will coach them as they practice until they can perform the auditory tasks at high frequencies. This intervention usually results in high frequency performance of auditory tasks whenever they appear in the regular curriculum.

At Morningside, we've found that employing learning channels, setting realistic goals for their acquisitions, and developing teaching protocols appropriate to each channel results in learners who acquire the entire range of skills needed to navigate in academic and life circles. It also teaches learners a valuable lesson about their ability to learn. Learners sometimes bring histories of having avoided certain kinds—channels—of tasks—and may initially resist instructional efforts to remedy their channel deficits. But resistance is fairly short-lived. While we've seen individual differences in the ease with which learners acquire different channels, our data provides compelling evidence that, in the very great majority of cases, learning is a function of the elegance of the instructional program and not of some physiological or genetic predisposition of the learner. We find that how students have been taught and what the expectations for learning have been in the past dictate how easy or challenging it will be for them to acquire particular learning channels. Most important, we find that a learning channels approach produces learners who are independent of arbitrarily-imposed boundaries.

Table 5 shows the learning channels associated with tool and component math, reading, and writing skills at Morningside.

Designation of learning channels allows the instructional programmer to ensure that all combinations required to operate effectively in authentic tasks are included in the instructional regimen. They also remind instructors that performance extension, commonly called "generalization," within and across learning channels is not automatic. Some economies do arise within and between channels. For example, individuals may learn to apply increasingly effective strategies to master each successive see/say or hear/write task. They may also find it easier to learn a new channel for specific content when they have achieved high levels of mastery in another channel. For example, a learner that can see/say numbers fluently is likely to find it easier to master see/write numbers than one whose performance on see/say numbers is still halting. Still, additional practice is almost always required in an unfamiliar or unpracticed channel to bring it to levels of mastery that Morningside promotes.

Table 5. Examples of Learning Channels in Math,
Reading, and Writing

Math	Reading	Writing
See/write math facts	See/say prose, text	Hear/write & hear/type letters, words, spelling (dictation)
See/say place value of a digit in a number	Hear word/write definition	See/write letters, words, notes (transcription)
Hear/write numbers (dictation)	See/write comprehension exercises	See short sentences/write combinations, applying grammar, usage, punctuation and capitalization principles
Think/say arithmetic solutions (mental arithmetic)	See/say text plus think/say: apply comprehension strategies	Think/write persuasive paragraphs

Haughton also promoted the use of learning channel matrices, a set of cells with stimuli on the vertical axis, responses across the horizontal axis, and cells in which to write examples of practice exercises in the intersecting channel. The learning channel matrix helps ensure that an educational program provides adequate opportunities for children to practice in a wide variety of channels. Preschool teachers under Haughton's tutelage would develop activities for unit themes by filling as many cells in the matrix as possible (see Figure 2).

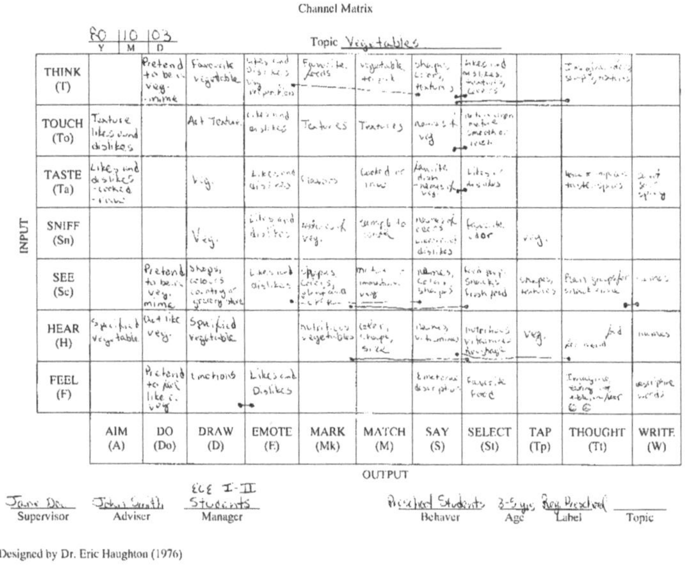

Figure 2. A learning channel matrix completed by students of Dr. Eric Haughton.

Morningside teachers are intentional in testing empirical questions that arise from the emphasis on learning channels on a case-by-case basis. Morningside's Precision Teaching system of continuous measurement, described in chapters 4 and 5, tracks patterns of growth within and across learning channels and also provides evidence about which instructional protocols most efficiently produce mastery.

Learning Outcomes. Morningside analysts rely on Tiemann and Markle's analysis of learning outcomes which first appeared in their 1983 text, *Analyzing Instructional Content* (see Figure 3). Tiemann and Markle's typology is reminiscent of Gagne's types of learning first described in his seminal work, *The Conditions of Learning* (1965, 1970, 1977, 1985). Gagne differentiated among five different types of learning or learning outcomes—verbal information, intellectual skills, cognitive strategies, motor skills and attitudes—on the basis of differential instructional protocols that each required. Tiemann and Markle's account extends Gagne's work, provides a different classification scheme that is somewhat more teacher friendly and, most important, includes extensive training in how to develop instructional protocols that result in the speediest acquisition of each.

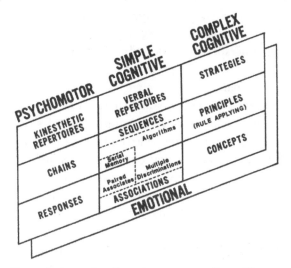

Figure 3. A matrix of learning outcomes. From Tiemann & Markle (1983, 1990).

Nine learning outcomes are proposed, three psychomotor skills, three simple cognitive skills, and three complex cognitive skills. *Psychomotor skills* are those in which the learner learns *how* to respond; these learning outcomes occur at the musculature level and emphasize the precise form of the response. In most instruction at Morningside, the necessary psychomotor repertoire already has been established, although there are exceptions such as becoming fluent with a computer keyboard or a mouse. In contrast, teachers in a typical preschool classroom would allocate a considerable amount of time to shaping response topographies such as shoe-tying, marking with a pencil, cutting with scissors, and stringing beads.

Simple cognitive skills include relatively straightforward stimulus-response relations that describe what goes with what, verbal chains and sequences, or the conditions that call for a certain response. Examples range from telling the capital of each of the United States, to reciting Martin Luther King's "I Have A Dream" speech, to describing an event you have just witnessed to a friend. They are simple only in the sense of being foundational.

Complex cognitive skills are those in which the learner responds functionally to novel stimuli or novel situations on the basis of critical features that embody all members of a certain class of stimuli or situations. Examples include concept learning and categorization, using a formula to calculate the area of a rectangle (principal applying), and deriving a strategy to solve a difficult problem for which no formula exists (contingency adduction).

Morningside's programs focus primarily on simple and complex cognitive skills.

Table 6 illustrates some common educational tasks for simple and complex cognitive skills according to Tiemann and Markle's learning outcomes typology. Within the simple cognitive column, Morningside prepares instructional scripts that teach associations, sequences, and verbal repertoires.

Table 6. Examples of Each of Tiemann and Markle's Simple Cognitive and Complex Cognitive Learning Outcomes

Simple Cognitive Skills	Complex Cognitive Skills
Associations	Concepts
Say the meaning of map symbols	Given a set of sentences, circle the noun.
Tell the capitals of the states of the United States.	Identify a book correctly according to category, for
Tell the meaning of metric prefixes (deca, kilo, mega, giga, etc.)	example, biography. Identify the artist of a piece of art you've never seen before.
Say the name of letters of the alphabet.	Identify the musical style of a piece of music.
Say the Japanese equivalent of a series of English words.	Differentiate word problems as cases of addition and cases of
Complete a page of addition and subtraction facts.	subtraction.
Name six impressionist artists.	Classify verbs according to tense. Tell what style is represented in a particular sculpture.
Tell the meaning of Latin abbreviations in reference citations.	Differentiate between synonyms, homophones, and antonyms. Differentiate between bacteria and viruses.
Sequence Learning	Principle Application
Say the letters of the alphabet in order.	Use a map to go to a location. Find a location using map guide
Repeat "I before E except after C."	letters and numbers.

continued...

Say the Pledge of Allegiance.
Count from 1–10 in Spanish.
Tell the formula for mixing a particular color of paint.
Repeat the formula for finding standard deviation of a set of numbers.
Tell the order of succession to the presidency of the United States.

Plot a point using Cartesian (x and y) coordinates. Convert Fahrenheit to Celsius.
Convert inches on a map to miles on the ground.
Use a map to find the shortest walking path between two points.
Use a map to find the shortest walking path between two points.
Convert between English and metric measurement.
Correctly punctuate a sentence.
Find the hypotenuse of a triangle given the opposite and adjacent sides.
Match the number of the subject and verb in a sentence.
Given a stroke volume and cardiac rate, calculate the cardiac output.

Verbal Repertoires

Tell how to take a person's blood pressure.
Retell the story of "Much Ado About Nothing."
Give a live report of an emerging crisis.

Strategizing

Determine how goods will be distributed fairly among a group of people.
Write a creative play.
Develop a recycling system that meets the unique needs of your community.
Predict what will happen to the price of fruit when a deep freeze destroys a substantial portion of the fruit crop.

Associations are specific stimulus-response pairs in which a particular stimulus occasions a particular response. In a history class, learners may draw associations between dates and events. In chemistry, they may learn to associate symbols with chemical elements or may learn to name a chemical compound when presented with its formula. That these are called *simple* skills and don't require much thinking does not mean they are easily taught or easily learned. For example, memorizing the names of all the nerves in the head has produced sleepless nights for many medical students. In fact, a great deal of psychological research has been directed toward identifying optimal teaching and practice routines to perfect these *simple* skills.

In *sequence learning*, a series of associations occur in a prescribed order. Sequence learning can be of two kinds—serial memory and algorithms. In serial memory, each response becomes a stimulus for the next response, and the responses flow continuously without interruption. For example, the learner says the alphabet in order, repeats the Declaration of Independence, provides a verbatim definition of homeostasis in biology, or says the lines of a play in drama class. Algorithms are step-by-step procedures that guide the performance of an already known set of responses. One learner tells another the steps to create the color mauve in an art class or tells how to create a table in Microsoft® Word. Students could also demonstrate sequence learning by retelling a story in memorized order. In *verbal repertories*, learners draw from a number of sources to talk about a topic at length and in depth in an order that changes every time. Instead of simply giving a memorized definition of homeostasis, they may define it somewhat differently, but correctly, each time. They may expand on the definition by giving examples, one on one occasion and a different one on another occasion. For example, color announcers on a baseball team are known for the many

49

different ways in which they can describe a line drive or a fastball. Story or passage retelling may vary from one telling to the next and still be complete, orderly, and exciting each time told. Improvisational acting is an example of a motor skill and simple cognitive verbal skill combination that draws upon rich verbal repertoires about all manner of topics.

Within the complex cognitive column, Morningside programmers differentiate among concepts, principle application, and strategizing. In *concept learning*, the learner comes to respond to critical features that determine categorical membership of stimuli that contain varying features irrelevant to their classification. For example, learners can distinguish examples of circles from among other shapes regardless of the size, shape, or color of the circle. They can distinguish between relative concepts such as more than and less than or same as and different than. They can distinguish between socialism and democracy. They can differentiate between two writing genres by finding examples of each. In *principle application*, the learner applies familiar algorithms or formulae to novel data or circumstances. Sometimes colloquially referred to as problem solving, it might more appropriately be thought of as rule following, saving problem solving for less well-defined "figuring out." For example, a learner may use a formula to find the temperature in Celsius given a temperature in Fahrenheit, mix a particular color of paint with a formula, or write a persuasive essay on the coming election according to specific features in a writing rubric.

All of the foregoing kinds of learning can be well-defined as tasks requiring facts, algorithms, concepts, principles and skills. Strategy learning is different. It is not well-defined in advance of execution.

Strategy learning is akin to the formal definition of problem solving in that it requires the learner to develop a solution to a problem for which a formula is not provided. For example, a learner might be asked to discover the formula to convert Fahrenheit to Celsius by examining pairs of temperatures in both scales. Or he may be asked to figure out how to mix a color of paint to match the pillows on a couch or solve an urban planning problem that no one before has been able to solve. No formula is provided, and contingency adduction produces an acceptable solution.

Morningside's content analysts identify the learning outcomes of each skill in each skill pyramid in the content area. They also identify the range of learning channels that match real-world expectations. Based on their understanding of these two content-independent characteristics of the learning objectives, instructional protocols are developed. Tiemann and Markle's protocols provide a beginning point for design.

The instructional protocol matched to each type and channel of learning becomes a kind of authoring system into which new content can be entered, producing a more or less explicit script for teachers to follow in facilitating the learners' progress. That is, one authoring system can be used to create scripts to teach any kind of association, regardless of the curriculum strand from which it's drawn, and at any level of difficulty. Another authoring system would be appropriate for all lessons that teach sequences, and still others would be required to teach concepts or principle application.

Although instructional designers initiate much of this design work, Morningside certified teachers begin to detect the characteristics that apply to different learning outcomes and learning channels as they acquire experience with different instructional scripts and protocols. When this exposure is combined with explicit instruction in content analysis and instructional design, teachers begin to develop their own analysis and design skills and become less dependent on tightly scripted lessons.

CHAPTER 4
USING A MULTI-LEVEL SYSTEM OF ASSESSMENT TO
INFORM INSTRUCTIONAL DECISIONS AND
DETERMINE PROGRAM EFFECTIVENESS

Susan Malmquist[7]

The Assessment System

A hallmark of Morningside procedures is the continuous interplay between instruction and assessment. The primary purpose of assessment at Morningside is to ensure that students are correctly placed in an instructional program and that they are making gains that promise long-term academic benefit. A multi-level system of assessment is used to best capture the effects of the academic program at Morningside Academy. The different levels of the assessment system represent *macro (once or twice yearly)*, *meta (weekly or monthly)*, and *micro (daily)* levels of assessment.[8]

Macro-Level Assessment

Published, Norm-Referenced Achievement Tests. The first level of assessment, the macro level, includes the use of published, norm-referenced or criterion-referenced tests. The results are used to gauge a learner's performance level in

---

[7] Dr. Malmquist has a private practice specializing in learning solutions for children, families, and schools. She also serves as an adjunct psychology professor at Central Washington University. She spent several years working at Morningside Academy as School Psychologist (1995–2001) and Assistant Director (2001–2002). She currently provides consulting services to the Morningside Teachers' Academy.

[8] Special thanks to Michael Fabrizio for applying the terms macro, meta, and micro to the assessment levels.

relation to peers at the beginning and end of the school year and to evaluate performance improvements using widely accepted measures of achievement. Students who participate in Morningside programs are routinely administered these tests at the beginning and end of a course of study. Because of varying national, state, and local testing requirements, different tests have been used at different implementation sites. *The Iowa Tests of Basic Skills* (ITBS), *Woodcock-Johnson Tests of Achievement III* (WJ-III), the *Canadian Test of Basic Skills* (CTBS), the *Metropolitan Achievement Test* (MAT), and the *Stanford Achievement Test* (SAT) are commonly used instruments for school-aged children. In Washington State, where Morningside Academy is located, students complete the *Washington Assessment of Student Learning* (WASL) in grades four and seven.

Published norm-referenced achievement tests are used for several reasons: (1) to obtain independent performance results on widely accepted measures used across the country, (2) to gain a sense of a student's entering basic academic skill repertoire at an emerging composite skill level, and (3) to determine shifts in performance after completing a course of study at a Morningside site. By using tests that are familiar to school personnel and other educational professionals, we are able to have a common reference point to discuss student performance. This is especially useful when coordinating with other schools and intervention specialists.

Additionally, the information obtained from the pre-test administration gives us an initial understanding of a student's overall academic skill level compared to typical peers. We consider these test data when we begin to look at instructional placement. While these tests do not typically probe with enough specificity or provide an adequate range or number of items to allow for good instructional planning decisions, they can tell if a student is performing in the average, above average, or below average range when compared to peers.

Table 7. Components of the Morningside Multi-Level System of Assessment

Assessment Level	Examples	Frequency of Measurement	Sensitivity to Growth Over Time
Macro	Published, Norm-Referenced Achievement Tests	Twice Yearly	Lower
	Morningside Precision Placement Tests	Once Yearly	N/A
Meta	Curriculum-Based Measurement	Weekly	Very High
	Portfolio Assessment	Monthly	High
Micro	Precision Measurement	Daily	Very High

Moreover, the results from the pre-test and post-test administrations can be compared to evaluate larger shifts in performance. When students increase their performance commensurate to typical peers in a given school year, this can be considered to represent one year's growth in one year's time. On a norm-referenced test, this would result in a percentile rank that stayed the same from one year to the next. To illustrate, if a student had a percentile rank of 50 in the spring and made one year's growth in the following school year, the student's percentile rank the following spring would still be 50. Many, if not most, of the students who are enrolled in Morningside programs have a school history that does not include such performance. They enter Morningside with school performance that has often stayed the same year after year or that has resulted in six months growth relative to peers in a given school year. This would result in percentile rank scores that drop from year to year, indicating that the gap between the student and his or her peer group is widening. In many instances, this poor performance is attributed to internal traits or characteristics of the learner (i.e., dyslexia, ADHD, sensory integration disorder), rather than to an interaction between the learner and the environment. At Morningside, the label will sometimes tell us about the type of intervention that will be most effective with a student, but we don't allow it to establish artificial ceilings on student achievement. As a result, these troubling outcomes can be dramatically altered for students who enroll in a Morningside program.

Once a student has fallen behind, it is necessary to achieve more than one year's growth in a year to begin to close the gap between the student and typical peers. When teachers fully and reliably implement Morningside programs, it is not uncommon to see students achieve two year's growth in a year on published, norm-referenced achievement tests. This is true even among students whose entering repertoires place them well below same age peers. At Morningside Academy in Seattle, parents are offered a money-back guarantee if their child does not achieve expected gains on standardized measures.

Diagnosis and Placement. Also included in the macro level of assessment are the diagnostic/prescriptive placement tests that are used to ensure correct instructional placement for students at Morningside. These Morningside precision placement tests are a critical part of the program because the speed with which students can complete a course of study is dependent, at least in part, on the accuracy of their program placement. After examining the results from the published, norm-referenced tests, more information is needed to determine correct program placement. A series of diagnostic/prescriptive placement tests, developed at Morningside Academy, are used to gain a better understanding of a student's skill strengths and weaknesses. An evaluation is completed of the component level skills missing from a student's repertoire. Students are then placed into homogeneous instructional groups and the most appropriate sequence of instruction is determined.

Meta-Level Assessment

Curriculum-Based Measurement. Morningside also tracks progress on important learning outcomes throughout the year using an adaptation of Curriculum-Based Measurement (CBM) procedures (Deno, 1985; Shinn, 1989). CBM is a set of standardized frequency-based measurement procedures used to evaluate student performance in basic academic skills, such as reading, written expression, spelling, and math. CBM was initially developed to provide teachers with reliable, valid, and efficient procedures for obtaining student performance data to evaluate their instructional programs and to make data-based decisions in an ongoing fashion.

CBM was formalized as a specific type of curriculum-based assessment in the 1970s after years of research conducted at the University of Minnesota (Deno, 1992). The conceptual underpinnings of CBM are grounded in the work of applied behavior analysis, with the use of single-subject data-analysis methodology and frequency as the key unit of measurement (Skinner, 1953), and in Precision Teaching, with the application of this work to the measurement of samples of behavior reflecting important academic skills (Lindsley, 1971). The impetus for the movement toward this system of "alternative assessment" developed in response to the problems associated with the sole reliance on published, norm-referenced IQ and achievement tests for making important educational decisions affecting students' lives. Briefly, some of the primary concerns with the over-reliance on traditional assessment measures have included: (1) their lack of utility in effective treatment planning, (2) often inadequate technical characteristics to support the educational decisions being made (e.g., special education eligibility, instructional planning, program effectiveness), (3) frequent misuse of scores, such as the ubiquitous grade equivalent score, (4) their use as a sole means of classifying children as handicapped, and (5) the contributions of traditional assessment measures to minority overrepresentation in special education programs with, often times, questionable effectiveness (Shinn, 1998).

CBM emphasizes basic academic skills monitoring in academic areas such as reading, writing, spelling, and math using short-duration, parallel, alternate forms. Brief assessments, usually no more than three minutes in length, have proven to be reliable and valid measures of general student achievement (Shinn, 1989). The primary focus is on long-term or annual goal measurement. The annual goal can be determined by examining baseline performance, normative performance, and commonly accepted standards for skill mastery, such as in reading (Carnine, Silbert, & Kameenui, 1990; Lovitt & Horton, 1991). Knutson and Shinn (1991) point out that the procedures are *curriculum-referenced* because assessment materials are drawn from and reflect the school's curriculum. They can be *norm-referenced* in the sense that local districts can develop local norms by collecting and comparing data on many students. And last, CBM provides for *individually-referenced* assessment because each student's performance can be compared at different points throughout the year to reveal individual growth.

The use of CBM allows for measurement that is highly sensitive to growth over time. These measures can be thought of as DIBS, Dynamic Indicators of Basic Skills (Shinn & Bamonto, 1998). They are *dynamic* in the sense that formative evaluation is used, with precise evaluation of on-going and dynamic changes in student behavior. CBM data serve as *indicators* of behavior because small samples of behavior are taken which serve as indicators of the larger, composite skill repertoire. Finally, the emphasis is on *basic skill* measurement because these skills are so critical for school success.

The most common CBM measures are in reading, written expression, spelling, and math. The assessments have an explicit set of administration directions that remain constant, the time component is kept the same from week to week, and performance is scored according to explicit criteria that are used among all those who use Curriculum-Based Measurement (Shinn, 1989). In this sense, CBM represents *standardized* assessment. Morningside employs the following CBM assessment tools:

- Oral Reading Fluency
- Written Expression
- Math Computation
- Math Concepts and Applications

These CBM measures are included as part of Morningside's entry assessment battery. The data they provide guide instructional placement decisions and serve as baseline performance measures that are useful for academic goal setting. After students have been placed in groups and instruction has begun, Morningside teachers administer CBM tests once a week in Written Expression, Math Computation, and Math Concepts and Applications. A Morningside support staff member collects the individually administered CBM Oral Reading Fluency data on a weekly basis. The CBM test results are charted, and the teacher, parent, and student can monitor progress toward an annual goal. Students receive feedback on their performance as well. This feedback keeps the students involved in their learning outcomes and provides a great source of motivation for both students and teachers alike.

CBM results are used to help guide instructional decisions throughout the school year. Morningside teachers are able to closely monitor the progress of students in a given instructional program. CBM data are analyzed on a monthly basis. If a student is making enough progress to meet the annual goal, the classroom teacher continues with the current blend of instructional elements. If however, the student does not progress as expected, an instructional change would be warranted. As necessary, teachers work with Morningside consultants to determine the instructional change most likely to improve performance. An evaluation of the CBM trend data provides meaningful clues as to the best blend of instructional technologies for various learner repertoires. These data form an important foundation for the empirical validation of instructional procedures at Morningside.

CBM Reading. In reading, student levels of Oral Reading Fluency are assessed on a weekly basis. Oral Reading Fluency materials are available for a variety of commonly used basal reading curricula, including Scott Foresman, Macmillan, and SRA's *Reading Mastery*. For this measure, the student reads aloud for one minute from three different passages randomly selected from the same measurement level. The number of words read correctly and errors are calculated. The passages are scored immediately by the examiner and summarized on the

Standard Celeration Chart. The administration and scoring time for each student is approximately 5 minutes per week. This measure provides for a very reliable and valid snapshot of a student's basic skills in reading. While it is clear that this measure evaluates oral reading proficiency, Marston (1989) provides evidence that oral reading fluency is also predictive of comprehension skills. A factor likely contributing to this relationship is that a halting reading style with many errors may make it difficult to understand the text.

Typically, students are monitored in CBM Oral Reading Fluency using tests that represent their grade level. At Morningside, this may or may not be the case. The appropriate measurement level is selected using the student's baseline performance. Some students may benefit from "out-of-level" testing because weekly measurement from their grade-level material would likely lead to frustration. Also, if the test is too difficult, improvements may go unnoticed. Therefore, it is important to select a measurement level that will be sensitive to growth, but at the same time, is as close to the student's chronological grade level as possible. When out-of-level testing is conducted, rapid progress will allow for jumping measurement levels throughout the school year. For example, if a fifth grade student begins the school year with measurement from the third-grade level, he or she would be able to enter the fourth, then fifth grade measurement levels as progress is noted. The opportunity to move back and forth across grade level measurements makes CBM Oral Reading Fluency highly sensitive to small increments in growth that are more difficult to spot in many other formative measures. The use of CBM Oral Reading Fluency represents high impact assessment. We have yet to find another reading test that yields so much information in such a short amount of time. A great deal can be learned about a student's overall reading skills with this one-minute snapshot.

CBM Writing. In writing, students are given a story starter and three minutes in which to write a narrative story. The Total Words Written (TWW), Words Spelled Correctly (WSC), and Correct Writing Sequences (CWS) are calculated. Total Words Written is a measure of a student's writing output, or how much a student can produce during a timed opportunity. Words Spelled Correctly provides a measure of spelling proficiency. Finally, the Correct Writing Sequences scoring metric is a measure of writing quality. For this score, correct spelling in context, correct use of grammar, and accurate punctuation, syntax, and semantics are required (Marston, 1989). A database of over two hundred story starters has been compiled at Morningside. The story starters can be teacher or student generated, but they must meet certain criteria for acceptability in generating a good story. For example, story starters that easily yield a yes/no response are unacceptable. For each administration, a different story starter is used, while the timing component and scoring rules stay the same. The administration takes about five minutes of class time per week. Teachers spend, on average, 30 minutes per week scoring the writing samples and managing the data on Standard Celeration Charts for a class. Student progress in writing can be seen readily using this measure. CBM Written Expression samples taken from one child in September and again in April of the same school year depict the tremendous improvement that is common for Morningside students.

The Written Expression samples in Figures 4 and 5 are from a second-grade student. At the beginning of the year, the student had considerable difficulty writing at a level that would be expected of an entering second-grader. In fact, this student had very few reading skills as well. These skill deficits would make it very difficult for him to keep up and meet the demands of a typical second-grade classroom.

Figure 4. A fall CBM writing sample from a
Morningside student.

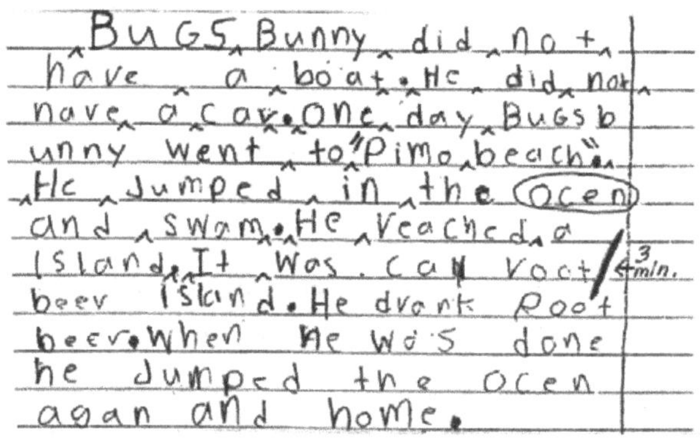

Bu GS Bunny did no t
have a bo at. He did not
have a car. One day Bugs b
unny went to Pimo beach.
He Jumped in the Ocen
and swam. He reached a
Island. It Was. Call Voot
beer Island. He drank Root
beer. When he was done
he Jumped the Ocen
agan and home.

Figure 5. A spring writing sample from the same
Morningside student.

Instructional programs were put in place to address the
deficits in writing and reading. Progress was monitored on a
weekly basis, using CBM. Data were evaluated on a monthly
basis and instructional modifications were made as needed.
The tremendous progress achieved is apparent. By the
following spring, he was able to write a story in three minutes
that was well within the range of what typical second-grade
students might produce under the same conditions.
Additionally, these CBM samples provide excellent social

validation. Parents, teachers, and other educators enjoy seeing these data "come to life" in conjunction with viewing the data depicted on a Standard Celeration Chart.

CBM Mathematics. In math, two different CBM formats are used. CBM Math Computation measures assess students' mastery of skills in addition, subtraction, multiplication, division, fractions, and decimals. CBM Math Concepts and Applications evaluates mastery of skills such as word problems, number concepts, charts and graphs, applied fractions and decimals, and measurement concepts. The test administration for each of these measures varies in length from two to seven minutes, depending on the measurement level. At Morningside, a computer-based application of CBM is used in math (Fuchs, Hamlett, & Fuchs, 1997). Students complete the tests in class using a paper and pencil version. Then, teachers enter the students' answers into a software program that automatically scores the test, charts the data, provides specific skill analysis, and aides in instructional decision-making. It typically takes no more than 30 minutes per week to enter scores for a class and manage the data.

An interesting side note is the effect on student performance of adding the computer-based application of CBM math concepts and applications (Fuchs et al., 1997). Historically, Morningside used Precision Placement Tests which did not include math concepts and applications measures. Even though instruction and practice were provided on concepts and applications, Morningside's Precision Placement Tests focused only on computation and word problem solving. Test scoring and data summary were completed by hand, and skill analysis was completed without the aid of a computer. When the computerized system made it less labor intensive for teachers to add concepts and application assessment to the CBM probes, students' yearly performance on this aspect of mathematics improved significantly.

Before instituting the computerized probes that included math concepts and applications, students' largest gains in mathematics on measures such as the *ITBS* were on the computation subtests. Within a year of using the computer-based system probes, students' performance on the problem solving and math concepts subtests of the *ITBS* quickly increased to levels comparable to the substantial computation improvements that had been typical of Morningside students. This provides evidence of the strength of the CBM math concepts and applications probes in modifying teachers' impressions of student growth and subsequently in the way mathematics is taught.

By utilizing a system of data based decision-making with CBM, teachers have confidence that they are using effective instructional procedures, students receive immediate feedback that they are learning, and parents are able to see evidence of the great impact of the Morningside program. Teachers and students both report that they enjoy using CBM in their classrooms. Teachers describe CBM as an assessment system that provides useful information in a teacher-friendly format that is easy to manage. Students actually look forward to their 'CBM time' each week, rather than experiencing the trepidation so often associated with test taking. Perhaps it is because they so clearly see the progress they make using CBM.

Portfolio Assessment

A popular assessment trend in education today is to document accomplishments with authentic student products, such as research reports, exceptionally completed homework, and personal graphs of books read per month (Shaklee, Barbour, Ambrose, & Hansford, 1997). We collect student work for portfolios at Morningside on a monthly basis and find these to be valuable supplements to our other data. A portfolio allows students, parents, teachers, and others to compare performance from September to June as well as throughout the school year. Pre- and post-school year compositions, tape recordings of oral reading, and the like can authentically illustrate remarkable progress and fit within a Deweyian spirit of real-world application and inquiry.

Micro-Level Assessment

Precision Measurement. By far the most important tool for the teacher in monitoring the effectiveness of instructional programs is Precision Teaching timing and Standard Celeration Charting (Graff & Lindsley, 2002; Lindsley, 1972, 1990; Pennypacker, Gutierrez, & Lindsley, 2003; see Figure 6). Precision Teaching is a fundamental approach in the Morningside Model of Generative Instruction. Several earlier references (Johnson & Layng, 1992, 1994, 1996) provide extended discussions of our comprehensive Precision Teaching technology.

Precision Teaching arose simultaneously with other mastery learning approaches in the 1960s and 1970s, but defined mastery differently. Whereas mastery was commonly defined in terms of performance accuracy, often 90 percent correct, Precision Teaching defined mastery in terms of rate of response. Morningside adopted Precision Teaching early on and has been a partner in its continued development.

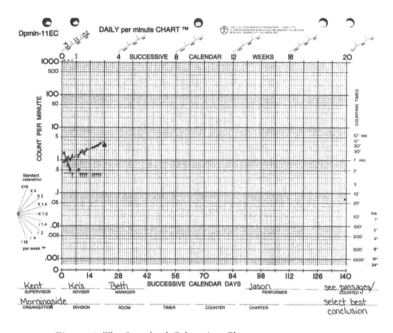

Figure 6. The Standard Celeration Chart.

Precision Teaching was conceived by Dr. Ogden Lindsley at the University of Kansas in his quest for a mechanism that brought continuous measurement and rate data into educational practice. Lindsley was heavily influenced by Skinner's allegiance to rate as the primary datum for studying behavioral change, and he recognized that traditional educational measurement systems that depend on percent correct and letter grades place artificial ceilings on performance and lead students and teachers to a false security about the strength of their performance. Both Skinner and Lindsley believed that high rate behavior not only looked different than low-rate behavior, it also had fundamentally different features. A student and colleague, Dr. Eric Haughton, developed the one-minute timing to track performance frequencies during practice (Haughton, 1972; Lindsley, 1972, 1990). Lindsley and Haughton promoted practice regimens that quickly produced high-frequency accuracy rates and low-frequency error rates on well-calibrated curriculum slices.[9]

At first, Haughton set performance frequency aims for learners that matched the rate at which an expert might perform a task, and learners practiced until the specified rates were achieved. As the theoretical understanding and pedagogical techniques of the approach evolved, a more sophisticated method for determining optimal performance rates and for achieving aims emerged. The acronym REA/PS— retention, endurance, application performance standards—was adopted, and precision teachers attempted to set desired performance frequencies that would predict these outcomes of skill acquisition at a later point in time.

In Precision Teaching parlance, once a performance demonstrates retention, endurance, and application, it is *fluent*. As a metaphor, performance fluency is flowing, flexible, effortless, errorless, automatic, confident, second-nature and masterful. When performance is fluent, it becomes a highly probable activity. Fluent performance is fun, energetic, naturally reinforced behavior. Dr. Carl Binder (1993, 1996) coined the term *fluency building* to refer to practice activities that are designed to achieve these goals. Currently at Morningside, we use five characteristics of performance to set fluent performance frequencies, changing the acronym to RESAA: Retention, Endurance, Stability, Application, and Adduction. Unless a frequency aim has been empirically demonstrated to produce the five characteristics of fluent performance, we use the term *frequency building* instead of fluency building.

---

[9] Within precision teaching, curricular strands are segmented into units, or "slices," for practice. Each slice provides multiple opportunities to respond to similar stimuli. Although some slices are independent of others in a curriculum strand, it is more typical that they are hierarchically arranged.

Fabrizio and Moors (2003) have recently demonstrated a promising empirical approach to verifying frequency aims as fluency aims by learning channels instead of resorting to the tedium of verifying each frequency aim as a fluency aim for each instructional objective. See Chapter 12 for an overview of this research.

The Standard Celeration Chart provides a picture of the learner's performance rate, error rate, and growth rate in a standardized format that allows teachers to make decisions at a glance about the learner's progress (see Johnson & Layng, 1992). As the name implies, precision measurement provides a system of data based decision-making that is very sensitive to fine increments of student growth. Teachers and students use these learning pictures on a daily basis to make decisions about what would be best for the learner to do next. Learning pictures provide information about how academically engaged time should be allocated in the classroom, when the curriculum step or slice is too large, and when the timing procedure requires modification. They reveal if the learner needs more instruction and practice in the current skill or if they need to drop back and become more firm on a previous slice of the curriculum. Sometimes, the student's performance suggests that the learner is ready to jump ahead in the curriculum. Teachers will, in these cases, probe performance on future slices of the curriculum or, if a probe suggests a need for it, they may provide an abbreviated instructional lesson. It's not at all unusual to find that the student already is at the prescribed frequency on subsequent slices without extensive instruction or more practice. At Morningside, in fact, contingency adduction is a way of life. Learner outcomes making up as much as one-third of a course of instruction emerge without direct instruction as the component skills that make up an emerging skill are mastered. Acquisition of these emerging skills, which the learner could not perform during baseline, is detected during routine probes. Students may need to practice the newly acquired skill to achieve desired frequency levels, but an explicit instructional program can be bypassed. See Chapter 6 for a more in-depth look at the Precision Measurement system used at Morningside.

A much more complete picture of student learning is obtained through the use of a multi-level system of assessment. The Morningside Precision Placement Tests help us to make good instructional placement decisions. Both the Precision Measurement and Curriculum-Based Measurement systems are highly sensitive to growth in component skills and inform instructional decisions on a daily, weekly, and monthly basis. The use of published norm-referenced tests (e.g., *ITBS*) and statewide assessment measures (e.g., *WASL*) captures the integration of these skills into composite skill repertoires and provides a measure of the degree to which component skills are being applied and composite skills adduced. Student work samples from the Portfolio Assessment system 'give life' to these data and illustrate the tremendous progress students can make using the Morningside Model. Together, these measurement tools serve not only to summarize student performance, but, in fact, help to actually increase student achievement in meaningful ways.

The Problem Solving Model

A decision-making framework helps guide the multi-level assessment system at Morningside. Rather than making decisions on a case-by-case basis in a random fashion, the use of a Problem Solving Model of student assessment provides a paradigm from which to view data based decision-making (Deno, 1989). Instead of administering the same test no matter what the presenting problem or situation, we are forced to ask, "What question am I trying to answer?" By examining this important issue, we are able to decide the relevant data that will help us make the best decisions about classroom placement and instructional programming. In this sense, academic assessment is viewed as *a process of collecting data to make important educational decisions* (Salvia & Ysseldyke, 1991).

The Problem Solving Model is predicated on important assumptions about the nature of how we view educational problems experienced by children and their families. The use of a Problem Solving Model assumes that the interaction between learner variables and environmental variables is of critical importance when attempting to intervene and provide support (Nelson & Hayes, 1986). While the physiological factors and learning history of the child merit careful consideration, there is a danger that they will become a convenient excuse for why the student isn't performing. When educators view the problem as the result of a static, unchangeable factor, such as IQ, or a disabling condition such as dyslexia, then, too often, low expectations are the result. When a problem solving approach is used, the focus shifts to *solving educational problems*. Within this model, the primary emphasis is placed on trying to identify and define the presenting problem, determine what resources and methods are most likely to yield improvements, and provide careful monitoring of treatment effects (Shinn, 1986; Shinn & Habedank, 1992).

The following is a description of the use of the Problem Solving Model within the Morningside Model, including how the various levels of the assessment system fit within this framework. The presenting questions, measurement activities, and important evaluation decisions are summarized below (see Table 8).

Table 8. Use of the Problem Solving Model with Assessment Data at
Morningside Academy (adapted from Deno, 1989)

Problem Solving Step	Presenting Question	Measurement Activities	Evaluation Decisions
Problem Identification	Does a discrepancy exist between the student's performance and that of typical peers?	Norm-referenced assessment	Determine how the Morningside Model will meet the student's needs
Problem Clarification	What is the student's entering skill repertoire?	Norm-referenced assessment Individually-referenced assessment	Determine classroom placement
Exploring Alternative Solutions	Which component skills require instruction? Given entering skill repertoire, what level of progress can be expected?	Specific-level assessment	Pinpoint blend of instructional elements needed Set annual goal and short-term objectives

continued...

Progress Monitoring	Is the instructional program effective?	Individually-referenced assessment	Determine whether student is making enough progress to meet annual goal
Problem Solution Determination	How do we program for skill application?	Individually-referenced assessment	Appropriate curriculum leaps, composite level instruction
	Does a discrepancy still exist between student and peers?	Norm-referenced assessment	Futures planning, transition plan

Problem Identification

The Problem Identification stage of the Problem Solving Model begins when a student is first enrolled in a Morningside program. For individual students who enroll at Morningside Academy, a careful screening process has already taken place to determine if there is a good fit between the child's needs and the Morningside program. The screening includes a parent interview, school tour, and a school visit in which the child participates in instruction at Morningside for at least one day. If the child is enrolled as a Morningside student, the formal Problem Identification steps begin with the administration of published, norm-referenced achievement measures. For other settings in which a Morningside program is used, the Problem Identification process begins with several meetings and interviews with school administrators and teachers to determine student and teacher needs. Then, norm-referenced assessment data that the school has for current students would be analyzed in addition to any supplemental norm-referenced evaluation conducted by Morningside consultants.

The primary purpose for collecting these data is to determine if a discrepancy exists between the student's performance and that of typical peers in skills such as reading, writing, and math (see Table 9).

Table 9. Problem Identification

Problem Solving Step	Presenting Question	Measurement Activities	Evaluation Decisions
Problem Identification	Does a discrepancy exist between the student's performance and that of typical peers?	Norm-referenced assessment	Determine how the Morningside Model will meet the student's needs

This gives us a sense of where to begin looking for appropriate classroom placement and instruction. For example, a student who falls into the average range in reading might need less instruction in component skills such as phonological coding and decoding, but may benefit from reading comprehension instruction. For a student who is performing well below average compared to peers in reading, a closer look at phonological coding, word attack, and language skills would likely be warranted. A student performing above average in reading compared to peers might do well in a higher-order reasoning program with advanced comprehension skills and an integrated literature and writing program. At this point, we are forming an initial hypothesis of what seems appropriate. Further assessment is needed for explicit instructional planning.

Problem Clarification
Problem Clarification is designed to provide a better sense of a student's academic skill repertoire (see Table 10).

Table 10. Problem Clarification

Problem Solving Step	Presenting Question	Measurement Activities	Evaluation Decisions
Problem clarification	What is the student's entering skill repertoire?	Norm-referenced assessment Individually-referenced assessment	Determine classroom placement

We examine the level of resources and instructional support needed to address any apparent skill deficits. First, the published, norm-referenced assessment results are compiled into a spreadsheet format for evaluation. Then, CBM data are collected to identify specific skill strengths and weaknesses. Typically, CBM measures at the student's chronological grade level are administered with the goal of collecting three baseline data points. As needed, CBM data at levels below or above the student's grade level are collected to determine the student's *independent*, *instructional*, and *frustration* levels of performance. The process of collecting CBM data at multiple skill levels is referred to as Survey-Level Assessment (Howell, Fox, & Moorehead, 1993). Next, Morningside Precision Placement tests are administered. These are un-timed tests that provide a solid basis for completing a component/composite skill analysis. The Problem Clarification procedures are norm-referenced because normative comparisons are used to aid in decision-making. The procedures are individually referenced as well, with a student's baseline performance serving as the starting point in determining individual academic goals.

After the CBM and Precision Placement data have been summarized and added to the spreadsheet database, the process of determining classroom placement and instructional groupings begins. Student groupings are formed based on similar instructional needs, with consideration of age. While mixed grade-level groupings are utilized, developmental levels and social needs play a role in determining instructional groupings. On a practical note, the number of instructional groups is related to the number of teachers who are available to provide instruction. At Morningside Academy, the typical student-to-teacher ratio is 8:1. In other sites, we strive for group sizes that are conducive to meeting the goals of a given instructional program. At times, some creative problem solving is used to recruit more teaching staff, including training instructional assistants and other school support staff to implement or support the program.

Morningside's entry-level assessment program has been fine-tuned over the years to become very efficient. Typically, between three-five school days are spent collecting these data. The time spent at the beginning of the program on Problem Identification and Clarification is a worthwhile investment that pays off in the long run, ultimately resulting in better learning for Morningside students.

Exploring Alternative Solutions

When instructional groups are formed, we have a good sense of which curriculum and instructional technologies will be blended together to form the classroom schedule. However, more information is needed to determine the exact level of the curriculum, and even lesson number, at which to begin instruction (see Table 11).

Table 11. Exploring Alternative Solutions

Problem Solving Step	Presenting Question	Measurement Activities	Evaluation Decisions
Exploring Alternative Solutions	Which component skills require instruction?	Specific-level assessment	Pinpoint blend of instructional elements needed
	Given entering skill repertoire, what level of progress can be expected?		Set annual goal and short-term objectives

At times, it is more efficient to begin at the mid-point of a given program in order to teach at the students' true instructional level, and therefore, reach optimal performance. It is during the Exploring Alternative Solutions stage of the Problem Solving Model that such Specific-Level Assessment is conducted. Specific-Level Assessment involves further probing into a student's skill repertoire. Often, this includes item analysis from assessment data that have been collected. Frequently, the specific placement tests that are included with a curriculum are administered as well.

Another activity that is completed during the Exploring Alternative Solutions stage of the Model is goal setting. CBM goals are set that reflect the progress that is expected by the end of the program of instruction, usually representing an annual performance goal. After the annual goal is set, short-term objectives are outlined as well. At Morningside, the annual goal is determined by examining the student's baseline performance and comparing it to typical performance for students at that grade level using local norms, instructional placement standards, or ambitious standards for growth based on expert judgment. An important part of the goal setting process is determining the measurement level materials for CBM Oral Reading Fluency, Math Computation, and Math Concepts and Applications. At times, this represents the student's chronological grade level. For students who are far behind, it often involves out-of-level testing. Again, if out-of-level testing materials are used, then the annual goal is usually written to include grade level jumps in measurement materials.

Short-term objectives are determined through an analysis of the annual goal and the number of weeks of instruction available. This provides teachers with a good sense of the progress that is needed on a weekly basis to maintain a trend in performance that will allow for the annual goal to be met. Standard Celeration Chart data from Precision Teaching fluency-building activities is used to outline skill objectives as well. By the end of the Exploring Alternative Solutions stage, operationally defined, measurable performance goals are set.

Progress Monitoring

Ongoing progress monitoring is the cornerstone of the multi-level assessment system at Morningside. The Morningside progress monitoring system is based on the principle of formative evaluation (see Table 12).

Table 12. Progress Monitoring

Problem Solving Step	Presenting Question	Measurement Activities	Evaluation Decisions
Progress Monitoring	Is the instructional program effective?	Individually-referenced assessment	Determine whether student is making enough progress to meet annual goal

At Morningside, formative evaluation involves successive hypothesis testing procedures using a single-subject time-series design (Deno, 1986; Sulzer-Azaroff & Mayer, 1977). Without such data, it would be very difficult to determine whether a given instructional intervention is working. The evidence in support of this model of formative evaluation becomes apparent when examining the traditional assessment model so commonly used in school settings. Frequently, program effectiveness decisions are based on post-test data from published, norm-referenced and criterion-referenced tests. In some circumstances, pre-test data might be available as well.

Several serious limitations prevent reliable and valid decision-making using these data. First, when assessment data come from norm-referenced measures, the results are not intended to measure individual growth over time. They are designed to provide normative comparisons between students. Even in a pre-test/post-test design, one can at best make normative statements at two different points in time. While the technical manuals written for these measures usually describe this purpose, misuses are common in both the educational and psychological literature. Second, a pre/post design does not provide information about what led to the improvements in performance that are seen. It is not possible to rule out other explanations for behavioral changes, including maturation effects (Deno, 1986). Finally, over-reliance on pre and post testing might lead to unwelcome surprises at the end of a school year. Without careful progress monitoring using formative evaluation and making program modifications as needed, it is not uncommon to find end-of-the-year test results that are disappointing. Unfortunately, what often happens then is that a school planning team tries to coordinate interventions for a student to occur for the following school year with a whole new set of teachers, often leading to a disjointed model of decision making. Deno (1986) aptly summarized this predicament with the conclusion, "The problem is, I think, that we collect not too *few*, but rather the *wrong* data."

The use of a system of formative evaluation at Morningside helps to address these problems. A student's CBM performance data are summarized on the Standard Celeration Chart. With these data, a true picture of individual student progress emerges over time. Trends in performance can be assessed and compared to expected growth, depicted as an annual goal, or aimline, on the Standard Celeration Chart. Data-decision rules are implemented to assist teachers in analyzing student performance over time. For example, if four consecutive data points fall below the aimline, then a program modification would likely be needed. To introduce an element of experimental control, teachers are asked to make one change at a time and to record it on the Standard Celeration Chart as a phase change. These phase changes help to discern which blend of instructional components is having the greatest impact on performance. When the student's performance consistently meets the aimline, the teacher has evidence to support the current program of instruction. Finally, if performance consistently exceeds the aimline, the annual goal and perhaps even the student's placement in the program would be re-examined.

By using this critical Progress Monitoring step in the Problem Solving Model, we are able to make finer grained instructional decisions. Within this framework, all of the elements of the Morningside Model work in conjunction and dramatic improvements in student learning can be seen. The lives of the children we teach are too important to leave such important outcomes to chance.

Problem Solution Determination

The Problem Solution step of the Problem Solving Model provides important information about what to do as performance improvements occur (see Table 13). CBM scores, Precision Teaching data, and other information collected during the course of instruction are used to decide when to make curriculum leaps.[10] Sometimes, only one or a few students in a group show evidence that they can make a curriculum leap. However, in other instances the entire group

---

[10] A curriculum leap, in Precision Teaching parlance, is a non-linear change in the student's placement in a program. The student "leaps" over the typical sequence to a place where his performance again requires instruction and practice.

can be moved ahead. Routine probing helps the teacher determine which of these two situations is the case. Plus, teachers learn to predict which slices of the curriculum are particularly susceptible to contingency adduction. This ability to make data-based decisions about when to skip instructional lessons is one of the secrets to success for Morningside teachers. In all cases, an important step before moving ahead in the curriculum is the shift in classroom activity toward application to ensure that component skills are firm in the context of composite repertoires and across settings, teachers, and materials.

Table 13. Problem Solution Determination

Problem Solving Step	Presenting Question	Measurement Activities	Evaluation Decisions
Problem Solution Determination	How do we program for skill application?	Individually-referenced assessment	Appropriate curriculum leaps, composite level instruction
	Does a discrepancy still exist between student and peers?	Norm-referenced assessment	Futures planning, transition plan

Another outcome of this process involves the movement of students between instructional groups as they progress at different rates. If a student moves at an accelerated pace compared to the rest of an instructional group, it might be time to look at instructional groupings again and give the student a chance to try more difficult material.

In addition to determining appropriate movement in the curriculum, the other primary decision during Problem Solution involves the evaluation of whether a discrepancy still exists between the student and his or her typical peers. To make this determination, norm-referenced and individually-referenced data are used. Throughout the school year, CBM and Precision Teaching data reveal meaningful patterns of growth. At the end of a school year or program of study, the alternate form of the selected norm-referenced achievement test is administered. When the time comes that a discrepancy no longer exists, students begin to receive instruction geared toward enrichment and continued fluent performance of skills recently acquired.

As a student becomes ready, a transition plan is created to help make the transition to a new school setting occur in a seamless manner. A team including the student's current teachers, parents, and school personnel from the new setting meet to make decisions about the appropriate next step for the student. An important team member in this process is the student as well. By examining the setting demands in the school planned for transition and comparing them to the student's current skill repertoire, we can greatly increase the likelihood of a successful transition from Morningside to a new school setting.

Following Sam[11] Through the Problem Solving Model

To help illustrate how the steps of the Problem Solving Model are used at Morningside, we will follow the progress of a fifth grade student, Sam, in math. These data are from Sam's third year of instruction at Morningside Academy in Seattle. When Sam first came to Morningside as a third-grader, he was experiencing difficulty with reading, writing, and math. During the first two years of enrollment, Sam showed the greatest progress in his reading and writing skills. While he progressed in math quite a bit the first two years, he still demonstrated some skill deficits in math when entering fifth grade.

Problem Identification

> Presenting Question: Does a discrepancy exist between the student's performance and that of typical peers?

Level 11 of the *ITBS* was administered in September to help determine Sam's math performance relative to his typical peers. The results are summarized below (see Tables 14–16).

The results from the *ITBS* show that Sam's overall math performance was in the below average range compared to other typical students entering fifth grade. He performed best on the Problem Solving and Data Interpretation subtest, with performance in the average range.

---

[11] Although the data presented here represent the work of a Morningside Academy student, the name has been changed to protect the confidentiality of the student.

Table 14. Sam's Fall ITBS Math Performance Results

ITBS Math	Standard Score	Grade Equivalent	Percentile Rank
Math Concepts & Estimation	182	3.6	20
Math Problem Solving & Data Interpretation	201	4.9	46
Math Computation	175	3.3	10
Math Total	186	3.9	21

His area of greatest difficulty appeared to be in math computation skills, with difficulty apparent in math concepts and estimation skills as well.

Table 15. Sam's Fall CBM Computation Scores

CBM Computation Scores	Digits Correct #1	Digits Correct #2	Digits Correct #3
Level 5	7	7	5
Level 4	12	14	12
Level 3	22	19	26

Table 16. Sam's Fall CBM Concepts and Application Scores

CBM Concepts & Applications Scores	Points #1	Points #2	Points #3
Level 5	7	6	3
Level 4	12	8	13
Level 3	21	18	24

While Sam still appeared likely to struggle in math without receiving specialized instruction, he had begun to close the gap between his performance and that of his peers. It was noted when reviewing Sam's file that his *ITBS* total math score from the year before showed performance at the 11th percentile.

Problem Clarification

More information was collected to help identify the best classroom group and instructional program to address Sam's math difficulty. At this point, CBM data and the results from the Morningside Precision Math Placement tests were examined. Three data points from the fifth grade CBM Math Computation and Math Concepts and Applications probes were collected. Data were collected from grade levels three and four as well. The CBM Math Computation scores are summarized in terms of the number of correct digits received, while the Math Concepts and Applications score is recorded as the number of points received during the timing period (see Tables 15 and 16). Precision Placement Tests were administered to evaluate whole number computation skills, fractions, decimals, and word problems.

> Presenting Question: What is
> the student's entering skill
> repertoire?

The Precision Placement test results were consistent with Sam's pattern of performance on the *ITBS* in the areas of computation and problem solving skills. However, more specific skill deficits were uncovered. Sam showed a skill strength in solving simple story problems that required the use of addition, subtraction, and multiplication skills. He did not demonstrate mastery of division, fractions, decimals, and even some longer multi-step multiplication skills. Data from the CBM Concepts and Applications tests were used to evaluate Sam's math concepts skills.

The CBM Math Computation results showed performance that was similar to the Precision Placement results. Sam attempted and appeared proficient in solving addition and subtraction problems, although one error in subtraction with regrouping was noted. He made several errors when attempting division problems, and a couple of errors in multiplication as well. He did not attempt any of the fractions problems, and put an X through these problems on the test. Sam showed difficulty in performance with the following math concepts skills: (1) number concepts, (2) grid reading, (3) charts and graphs, (4) measurement concepts, (5) area and perimeter, and (6) skills requiring applied fractions and decimals. He performed best in identifying names of numbers and math vocabulary terms. The results show that Sam was most proficient when tested at the third grade measurement level for both computation and math concepts skills. His instructional level appeared to be at approximately a fourth-grade level, with some skills typically mastered in third grade still not firm. The fifth grade level curriculum would likely represent a frustration level for Sam due to the high number of errors.

After evaluating these data in conjunction with the *ITBS* test results, the appropriate instructional group was determined. A preliminary decision was made to see if the students would benefit from one of the levels of *Saxon Math*, likely *Saxon 54*. Because this represented an ambitious instructional placement for Sam, it would be combined with an appropriate Precision Teaching component.

Exploring Alternative Solutions

After Sam was placed in a classroom group with other 4th, 5th, and 6th grade students with similar instructional needs, the specific blend of curriculum components was determined. First, students took the placement test for Saxon 54. They also began practicing important math component skills in a Precision Teaching format to evaluate entering performance relative to ultimate mastery standards.

> Presenting Question: Which
> component skills require
> instruction?

It turned out that Sam was not the only student in his class who had serious skill deficits in computation skills. Many other students had difficulty with these skills, especially with fractions and decimals. It was determined that the best course of action was to hold off on beginning instruction from the *Saxon 54* math program and focus instead on a diagnostic/prescriptive math program to improve component math skills. A goal was set to begin instruction from Saxon 54 in November. In the meantime, the teacher would use a diagnostic/prescriptive wall chart outlining skill objectives with each student's level of mastery summarized on the chart.

Explicit instruction and practice activities would be sequenced to best address the needs of each student in the group. Students would also learn to use the TAPS procedure in math and apply TAPS when solving word problems.

> Presenting Question: Given entering skill repertoire, what level of progress can be expected?

After examining Sam's baseline CBM performance, it was decided that his math progress would be monitored initially with the 4th grade level of CBM Math, for both Computation and Concepts and Applications. A goal was set that he would achieve 25 digits correct in Computation, and 25 correct points in Concepts and Applications, by January. Then, he would be bumped up to the 5th grade measurement level, with a goal in Computation of 50 digits correct, and 35 correct points in Concepts and Applications, by June.

Evaluating Solutions
Sam's progress was monitored weekly with CBM. Sam's teacher tracked the progress Sam was making and provided him with weekly feedback on his improvement. Additionally, she used the specific skill analysis data from the CBM computer programs to establish short-term objectives and to determine if students retained and applied the skills they worked on in class.

> Presenting Question: Is the instructional program effective?

In particular, Sam's teacher noted that he became much more proficient in multiplication and division skills, and began to attempt problems requiring the use of fractions and decimals. He still had the greatest difficulty with fractions, so this became a targeted area of further instruction and practice. After instruction with Saxon 54 began, Sam began to show mastery of number concepts, measurement concepts, and grid reading. Area and perimeter, grid reading, and applied fractions and decimals were slower to develop. Therefore, Sam's teacher reviewed these lessons and provided more applied practice on these skills. Sam's CBM Math Charts depict the growth he made over the course of the year (see Figures 7 and 8). The data illustrate that Sam made the greatest progress in math computation skills after five-minute math computation timings were added for fractions and decimals. His improvement in math concepts can be seen with the introduction of the *Saxon 54* program in November.

Sam was successful in reaching his mid-year goal using the 4th grade measurement level and switched to the 5th grade level as planned. Sam made steady progress from February to June, and ultimately met both of his annual goals.

Problem Solution Determination

> Presenting
> Question: How
> do we program
> for skill
> application?

As Sam began to demonstrate mastery of important component math skills, additional application activities were included so that he could receive further practice on these skills. For example, he used TAPS procedures independently across several different skill areas. Students in the class practiced measurement skills by measuring things in the classroom, school, and neighborhood and recording them in a journal. Sam also kept a journal of word problems he wrote that included fractions and decimals for other students to try and solve.

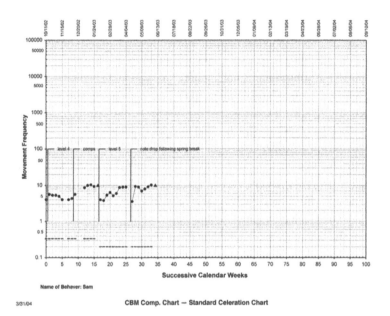

Figure 7. Sam's CBM math computation chart. Measurement from Level 4 depicts count per minute data from a three-minute weekly timing. Measurement from Level 5 depicts count per minute data from a five-minute weekly timing.

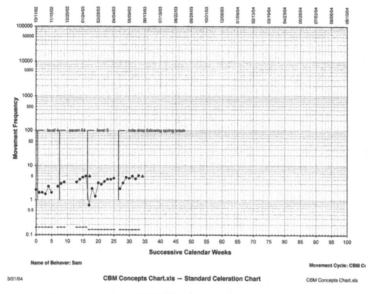

Figure 8. Sam's CBM math concepts and applications
chart. Measurement from Level 4 depicts count per
minute data from a six-minute weekly timing.
Measurement from Level 5 depicts count per minute
data from a seven-minute weekly timing.

In fact, many of these work samples formed the basis of Sam's
Math Portfolio. Sam's math journal, CBM test samples, and
Precision Teaching Charts were included as part of his
Portfolio Assessment in math. His teacher shared these work
samples during parent-teacher conferences to help illustrate
Sam's progress.

> Presenting Question:
> Does a discrepancy still
> exist between student
> and peers?

91

Table 17. Sam's Spring ITBS Math Performance Results

ITBS Math	Standard Score	Grade Equivalent	Percentile Rank
Math Concepts & Estimation	216	6.1	53
Math Problem Solving & Data Interpretation	222	6.4	59
Math Computation	219	6.4	59
Math Total	219	6.2	57

The alternate form of the ITBS was administered in June to help evaluate Sam's math skills. The results help capture the progress Sam made throughout the year (see Table 17). He ended the school year with performance in the average range on all of the *ITBS* math subtests, including his lowest area, Math Computation.

After discussing options for the next school year, Sam's parents decided they would like to enroll him in summer school to provide continued practice on his math skills. In addition, he enrolled in the summer "Budding Great Thinkers" program to further develop his critical reasoning skills. Sam's parents planned to enroll him for one more year at Morningside in the enrichment program to work on composite level skills as well as study skills. Then, after four successful years at Morningside, a transition plan would be created for Sam to enter his neighborhood middle school.

The use of the Problem-Solving Model embedded in a system of multi-level assessment provided a comprehensive evaluation of Sam's math performance. The macro-level of assessment was useful during Problem Identification and Problem Solution Determination, when a norm-referenced decision was made to compare Sam's math performance with that of his typical same-grade peers. The meta- and micro-levels of assessment were implemented during Problem Clarification, Exploring Alternative Solutions, and Progress Monitoring to create an instructional program for Sam. Together, these steps resulted in a multi-level system of assessment that helped to inform instructional decisions and determine program effectiveness. Not only did this system yield a summary of Sam's performance by helping to determine his progress each step of the way and clarify what he needed to work on throughout the school year, it helped to increase his math achievement as well.

CHAPTER 5
INSTRUCTIONAL PROGRAM DEVELOPMENT AND THE THREE PHASES OF TEACHING AND LEARNING

Instructional Design

Morningside designers follow the system of instruction described by Markle and Tiemann and presented in chapter 3. Their system promotes mastery, a core feature of the Morningside Model of Generative Instruction. We present the diagram of their system again in Figure 9. Follow the diagram closely as we describe the design process. Based upon specifications from the task and content analyses of the instructional objectives (see steps 1 and 2), we either develop our own instructional materials from scratch; or we select, enhance, and incorporate commercially available materials. Many instructional designers, both inside and outside of the behavioral community, have produced effective materials. The work of Siegfried Englemann and his colleagues is probably the best example, but we've also benefited enormously from the work of Dr. Anita Archer, Elizabeth Haughton, and Michael Maloney. John Saxon's math curriculum articulates especially well with Morningside Academy's teaching approach. Publishers of curricular series in reading and mathematics are increasingly attentive to the literature on instructional design and produce outstanding materials. The materials we adopt and adapt are listed in Table 1 in Chapter 1 of this book.

When otherwise promising, commercially available materials lack some of the empirically supported protocols for skill acquisition or don't include as many opportunities for practice as the Morningside Model prescribes, Morningside designers overlay instructional protocols or design additional practice to ensure that the materials meet the standards Morningside has adopted.

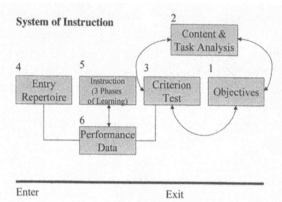

Figure 9. Markle and Tiemann's system of instruction. Adapted from Markle & Tiemann (1967).

The procedures we use to design an instructional program (see step 5) are based upon Markle's and Engelmann's design principles (see Markle's *Design for Instructional Designers*, 1990, and Engelmann and Carnine's *A Theory of Instruction*, 1982). In general, our designers, like these and other pioneers in the field, minimize teacher talk in favor of frequent, active learner responding. They strive for faultless communications in which one and only one message is likely. They favor lean, elegant programs that move learners from instructional routines to practice routines as quickly as possible. And finally they prompt the teacher to provide praise for correct student responses and describe corrective feedback for anticipated student errors.

Notice that an instructional program launches from some previously determined entering repertoire (step 4), and teaches the learner to perform in a manner specified by terminal objectives (step 1). The performance that indicates mastery of the objectives is illustrated in the outcome test (step

3). In other words, the program is designed to take the learner from one point in the curriculum to another. Programs typically contain several lessons that follow similar formats but with progressively advanced content. Within a single lesson, the authors may present several tool or component skills that don't have a hierarchical relation to each other but that, in parallel, form the foundation for some next level component or compound skill (see Engelmann & Carnine's multi-track lesson design, 1982).

Although a particular program may have designated entry and exit points, learners are not force-fit into an instructional program. Rather, instructional programs are implemented to fit the learner. All learners take an entry repertoire test (step 4) and an outcomes test (step 3) before studying a particular instructional program. One learner's performance on the entering behavior test may show a need for instruction on prerequisite objectives before studying the instructional program. Another learner's performance on the outcomes test may show that some of the objectives taught in the instructional program are already mastered or may require only practice. Instruction can be tailored to each learner within a relatively homogeneous group of learners accordingly.

There are no assumptions based on age or grade of the learner. Often corrective or remedial learners enter our instructional programs with some but not all of the skills that comprise content mastery. Such learners often are said to have "splinter" skills. For example, if a composite skill is made up of 10 component skills, a learner with splinter skills might have mastered skills 1, 3, 5, 7, 8, and 9, but not 2, 4, 6, and 10. The diagnostic/prescriptive regimen we adopt enables us to instruct where needed and skip segments of instruction when appropriate. Once pretesting establishes a general prescription about skills that need to be instructed or firmed, performance data collected during instruction (step 6) confirms when curriculum leaping or explicit instruction are appropriate.

Sometimes, Morningside designers encounter missing skills that are not a part of their instructional program. In such cases, they go back to work to find or establish additional lessons or program pieces that form a bridge between the learners' entering repertoires and the terminal goal.

An excellent case in point is the addition of explicit instruction in phonological coding to our reading curriculum options. Many reading programs begin with an implicit assumption that learners can hear, discriminate, and reproduce sounds, that sounds in isolation can be blended into words, and that words are heard as an ordered series of sounds. But we had noticed that our many of our beginning readers had not acquired these important skills, which often are taught informally in parent-child interactions or in day-care and preschool settings. Simultaneously, our colleague, Elizabeth Haughton, founder and director of the Haughton Learning Center in Napa, CA, was discovering the same thing. Informed by a review of research and armed with expertise in content analysis and instructional design principles, she designed a program that teachers can use to bring these important early reading skills to levels of fluency that makes them useful to more complex reading and language tasks. The Morningside team immediately incorporated *Phonemic Awareness: Phonological Coding* (Haughton, 1999), into its program options for learners for whom these skills needed to be directly taught or practiced. The result is that students who complete elements of the phonemic awareness program corresponding to their skill deficits then reenter our phonetic decoding programs and make speedier progress to fluency of their component elements.

Three Phases of Teaching

At Morningside subject matter is taught in instructional blocks made up of three primary activities: instruction, practice, and application. Each instructional objective or set of objectives is taught in these three phases. The instructional sequence identified in Markle's system of instruction (step 5) consists of these three phases.

Instruction

Instruction refers to *establishing a new repertoire*; the learner *acquires* a performance that she could not perform previously. Instructional programs teach associations, sequences, concepts, and principle applications and promote strategy learning (contingency adduction). The specific format of the lesson is a function of the learning channel and learning outcome of the task it is designed to teach (see chapter 3.)

Each instructional lesson is an interchange between the teacher and either a single learner, a small group of learners, or an entire class. Students engage with a teacher in highly interactive lessons that introduce one performance or skill at a time and cumulatively combine them as accuracy emerges. Dr. Tom Gilbert's mathetics model (1962a, 1962b) is the primary method for establishing new well-defined objectives. Establishing acquisition by using mathetics is equivalent to generalized imitation training. In mathetics, teachers *demonstrate* and *model* expected performance, *prompt* and *lead* students through the performance, and then *release* or *test* the student's performance. These steps in the mathetics process are easily identified during instruction, as teachers preface by saying "My turn" when they demonstrate and model, "Our turn" when they help the learners to perform accurately, and "Now your turn" when they check to see whether students can perform without assistance. Lessons are tightly structured, and their design is intended to produce the speediest possible acquisition of new skills, judged by the degree to which they match an expert's performance, in this case the teacher's performance or the "answer key." During this phase, the learner is quite dependent on prompts from the teacher, searches for clues to the correct performance, and displays some level of errors. Extraneous stimuli easily distract performance.

During instruction, students learn *how* to respond as well as *when* to respond. Critical discriminations are taught by blending Dr. James Evans' RULEG or EGRUL methods (Evans, Homme & Glaser, 1962) into mathetical design. In RULEG, teachers present "rules" or heuristics about how and when to perform, and then illustrate with examples and nonexamples. Teachers then lead and test students with examples and nonexamples until the learner can perform without assistance. In EGRUL, teachers present examples and nonexamples and lead students to derive rules and heuristics, in a structured kind of discovery learning. In technical language, the instructional program shapes response topographies and ensures discrimination among and stimulus control by novel and familiar stimuli. Student performance comes under the control of the parameters that define acceptable variability of stimuli and acceptable latitude for responses.

Many learners need a very explicit and structured version of mathetics to make rapid progress. These include (a) young learners, (b) older learners with deficient learning skills, (c) learners with learning and developmental disabilities, (d) learners whose backgrounds have underprepared them for academic learning, and (e) learners who encounter "brand new" content that allows for little transfer of training. For these learners, Siegfried Engelmann's Direct Instruction (DI) application of mathetics is very successful. During a DI lesson, teachers present lessons to learners that designers have scripted, word for word, in advance. The scripts take the utmost care to present a hierarchy of component and cumulative compound skills. The best DI scripts have been "learner verified"; that is tested with hundreds of learners in many settings and revised until they work. During a DI lesson, learners answer teacher-initiated questions and tasks in unison (see Carnine, Silbert, & Kameenui, 1990; Stein, Silbert, & Carnine, 1997). Teachers move through a series of questions and tasks in a predictable manner, provide attending cues to ensure that all learners are focused on the task, and signal learners to ensure that they respond together. Teachers may use a variety of signals; for example, tapping a pen on the overhead transparency or snapping their fingers, until they find one that works, is comfortable to use, and doesn't distract students. Teachers systematically vary the latency between the question and the response signal to ensure that the signal tightly controls responding.

Teacher and students volley many times a minute with their questions and answers. Teachers praise and correct student responses, providing parallel tasks until all students are accurate. Logically and empirically validated sequences lead students through nearly errorless learning in which stimulus discrimination is explicitly taught and response forms are shaped. The explicitness and careful progression of Direct Instruction lessons assures that students-at-risk develop flawless skills very quickly.

During the instruction phase, not only low-skilled learners but also inexperienced teachers profit from learning to establish new performances with tighter DI mathetics lessons. In the process of using DI scripts—which tell the teacher exactly what to say, how the learner should respond, how to predict errors, and how to provide error-correction procedures—teachers are explicitly shaped to establish skills.

This guidance ensures that the sequence and style of presentation conforms to the most efficient instructional protocols. Many of these protocols don't come naturally to teachers, and even the most experienced teachers find it difficult to craft effective protocols in real time. Teachers who are inexperienced with the theoretical and practical instructional design underpinnings of the Morningside model depend on heavily scripted programs to achieve procedural reliability in implementing instructional programs. As they gain experience with the instructional protocols that conform to each learning channel and learning outcome, however, they become less dependent on scripted lessons.

The challenge for the inexperienced Morningside teacher is to faithfully present the lesson as designed, achieve choral responding among learners, listen carefully to the quality of their responses, provide encouraging feedback following correct responses, and apply error correction procedures that effectively reduce errors. Even though teachers may consult the script during the lesson, they must be conversant enough with its pattern to maintain eye and ear contact with learners. The best results occur when teachers are able to implement programs with a great deal of procedural reliability, although the lessons are generally forgiving about small lapses in procedure.

Whether using tighter DI scripted or more generic mathetics lessons, teachers proceed through lesson in four stages. They verify, randomize, pace, and individualize opportunities to respond.

Verifying. First, teachers ensure that learners can respond correctly to a set of questions or tasks. During this phase, they provide "think time" before each question and provide prompts as needed to assure correct responding. They modulate up and down the continuum among modeling, prompting or leading, and testing, as student performance dictates. For example, the teacher may successfully prompt a performance and then try a test. If the student makes an error, the teacher would then back up and prompt the task again or might even model the performance prior to the next opportunity, then prompt some more. This dance continues until students can perform a test or release task successfully, without assistance.

Randomizing. After the verify stage, teachers randomize items to be sure that student performance is responsive to the task and not to its order of presentation. The teacher moves through the instructional items, for example, a word list, in an unpredictable order until performance under this condition is equivalent to performance under the ordered condition. This is a particularly important step in the process because without reshuffling, the item order itself may become a prompt or hint to the "right" answer. But for the learner to be able to engage in the skill in other situations in which it is needed, it has to be the instructional stimulus, not the order, that occasions the correct response.

Pacing. The teacher then picks up the pace, reducing the amount of "think time" in preparation for frequency building. Teachers build rate in this instructional phase until students are able to respond without hesitation. Teachers sometimes engage the student in a "paced race" in which an initial performance serves as a baseline for students to better. So, for example, if on the first try through a list of words, it takes 35 seconds for students to respond, the teacher might challenge students to complete the list in 25 seconds. This process continues until students reach a pre-established rate. On the word list example, students continue until they can respond chorally and correctly at a minimum rate of one response every two seconds. Over time, teachers and students know when that every-other-second pace has been achieved even without a stopwatch. They get the beat!

Individualizing. Last, the teacher provides individual turns to ensure that all learners have acquired the skill. Going back to the word list task, the teacher will say, "What word........Janelle?" To ensure that all students continue to attend to all possible items, the teacher always identifies the item first and then calls on the student. Teachers may make strategic decisions at this point about which students need the most opportunities and may, following an error and an error correction, return to the student who made the error later in the individualization stage and give him another opportunity to respond. Although Morningside certified teachers detect individual hesitations during choral responding, the individualization stage confirms their assumptions and may result in an individual mini-lesson for an individual student or two who hasn't kept pace with the group.

Throughout instruction, in addition to modulating the three aspects of mathetics (demonstrate, prompt, release), teachers directly address errors as they arise in other ways. Errors arise for different reasons and provide an opportunity to determine imperfections in the instructional lesson. As teachers develop expertise with programs, they detect an error, determine its probable cause, and provide an immediate and error-specific correction.

Let us clarify some different kinds of error-corrections to illustrate this point. In many cases, teachers recognize that a *lapse in procedure* has spawned an error, and they tighten their own procedure. Teachers may provide a specialized *attending cue* that focuses students on individual elements of the question they missed. If students are discriminating among vowel-consonant-vowel and vowel-consonant words and they are making errors, the teacher may *pre-correct* them by reminding them to look at the end of the word before responding. The teacher may also encourage students to look at the end of the word AND *remember the rule.* Alternatively, he may present an example and nonexample, side-by-side, that vary only on the critical element and encourage *discrimination*. For example, the teacher may present the words rat and rate and ask, "In which word will the vowel say its name?" Or, if the student says "rat" when the word is "rate," the teacher might write the word "rat" next to the word "rate" and say, "I heard rat. This word is rate." The teacher may also use a direct conversion procedure, changing the word from one form to another by erasing and substituting the key differences. She may use *build-ups* to assist the learner in perfecting a response. For example, if the learner is saying "cam" when the word is "cram," the teacher might cover the "cr" and ask, "What word?," and then unveil one letter at a time in backward order until the word is read correctly. Teachers might also *pre-correct* by saying, "Here's a word that has caused you trouble before. Look at it." Or they may pre-correct by beginning a lesson with some *tips and quips* to remind students to apply skills they've learned previously.

If it becomes apparent that several elements necessary for correct responding are missing for some or all students, the teacher may conduct a brief mathetics review lesson to firm up a tool or component skill or he may slice back to a point in the curriculum where performance stabilizes.

We've discussed the importance of tighter, DI scripted mathetics lessons for at-risk learners of all kinds, as well as for inexperienced teachers. More generic mathetics lessons to establish performances are actually most often appropriate. At least half or more learners have more advanced learning-to-learn skills than their at-risk peers. Most courses of study are not "brand new" experiences for a learner, although some foreign language and science courses are examples of exceptions. Each successive lesson overlaps with other lessons previously mastered; that is, they require entry repertoires already learned. Teachers also reach the point in training and practice where they have fluent generalized repertoires of effective instructional approaches. Instructional lessons for these students and with these teachers allow a shift to more generic mathetics approaches. Generic mathetics approaches still involve frequent exchanges between teacher and students, with praise and error corrections. They also contain model, prompt/lead, and test modulations until all students can perform successfully without assistance. However, students may encounter more teacher talk before responding, with the teacher thinking aloud to show how he formulates a successful answer to a task. For example, to teach a reading comprehension skill "making an inference," the teacher may define inference," read a short passage, and "think aloud" one or more inferences that can be drawn from the passage. Learner responses to tasks may also require lengthier answers. The teacher may read another short passage and ask students to make inferences and justify their answers. Unison responding may not be choral; teachers may give "think time" to students to write answers to such tasks, and then call upon a student or two to read their answers, while others check their answers against the feedback she provides. Students may also compare their written answers in peer pairs. The teacher may back up and provide more think-aloud models if the students are off-base. She may provide hints and otherwise lead the students to make more plausible inferences, and then read a new short passage and test the student's skill at making inferences. Many variations are possible. Mastery is still the learner's goal, and learner performance still drives the teaching, but the learner is expected to reach mastery with less explicit teacher shaping.

Thus, the programs that Morningside adopts represent a continuum from very formal, tightly scripted instructional programs that employ unison responding—for example, Engelmann's Direct Instruction, to semi-scripted programs—

for example, Anita Archer's *REWARDS* program, to programs in which teachers overlay mathetics on a completely unscripted program.

Both more formal DI lessons and more generic mathetics lessons have been designed to teach many complex skills in word problem solving, pre-algebra and algebra, chemistry, earth science, economics, history, logic and argumentation rules, and study skills, to name a few. A well-designed program makes learning difficult material as straightforward as learning simpler material.

Establishing and acquiring are the gateway to mastery and fluency, but they are not synonymous with it. The Morningside Model assumes that accuracy is only the first step in mastery. This belief is based on empirical evidence in the Morningside laboratory school. For example, students may not show retention until they reach a frequency aim. Many students cannot perform skills in September that they were taught in the previous spring term. An examination of their Standard Celeration Chart data from the previous June shows they did not reach the frequency aim before they took the summer off. In another article (Johnson & Layng, 1992) we presented a chart of another student who showed accuracy and retention but poor performance endurance until she practiced the skill to a higher frequency. Many learners who move from skill to skill with halting, if accurate, performance encounter greater and greater difficulty learning each subsequent skill. In the Johnson and Layng article we presented another chart showing a student who had difficulty mastering a compound skill, long division, until he practiced one or more of its component skills (math facts, rounding) to higher frequencies. Sam's charts in Chapter 4 also showed the need for fluency building. Hundreds of charts at the Academy illustrate the problem of teaching only to accuracy criteria. Accuracy teaching may not be sufficient for retention, endurance, stability, and ease of application and adduction. Thus, when prescribed levels of accuracy emerge, students enter the second, practice stage.

Practice

Following successfully completed instructional lessons; students in Morningside classes practice their freshly learned skills until they achieve levels of performance characterized by durability and applicability. Practice is timed, highly structured, goal-oriented, and continuously monitored. Practice sessions apply Precision Teaching technology. A brief history of Precision Teaching was included in Chapter 4. We provide a more detailed analysis of the influence of Precision Teaching at Morningside Academy in other published articles (Johnson & Layng, 1992, 1994).

Morningside students experience a hefty amount of practice, as much as 40 percent of their school day. Practice procedures are highly structured and fast paced, and practice requirements extend to all curriculum objectives. Morningside designers have developed practice activities on paper, on computer, and with flashcards for each major tool and component foundation skill in our curriculum. Teachers measure student performance on prescribed activities on a daily basis. Having fluent prerequisite skills makes learning subsequent, related skills faster and more successful.

In our peer coaching technology (Johnson & Layng, 1992, 1994) pairs of students practice building skills to frequency aims, although sometimes they practice alone or in threes. During practice, students time themselves on specially designed frequency-building materials until they can perform a certain amount—accurately, smoothly, and without hesitation—in a certain amount of time. Timings are usually 1 minute, but range from 10 seconds to 10 minutes. Students record their timed performance on Standard Celeration Charts

(Graff & Lindsley, 2002; Lindsley, 1972, 1990; Pennypacker, Gutierrez, & Lindsley, 2003).

Teachers set both performance and celeration aims. Performance aims tell the student how many of a skill they should be able to do in the timing period. We have set desired rates somewhat arbitrarily on the basis of rates that conform to what skilled adults can do and that appear in practice to be associated with the main characteristics of fluency: retention, endurance, stability, ease of application, and likelihood of occurrence in a contingency-adduced repertoire. However, as we discuss more fully in Chapter 12,

- most of these rates have not been empirically tested.
- there is still some possibility that number of trials instead of rate or some combination are responsible for producing characteristics of fluency.
- it is unclear if content, learning outcome (Tiemann & Markle, 1983, 1990), or learning channels (Fabrizio & Moore, in press) or some combination would be the basis for prescribing ideal performance rates.

Currently, we expect students to be able to decode words at 80–100 a minute, find 8–10 main ideas in paragraphs in three minutes, compute fractions at 60–80 steps a minute, complete 12–15 arithmetic word problems in five minutes, combine five short sentences in 30 seconds, and so on. Celeration is a measure of the change in rate over time and indicates whether the student is reaching a performance aim in a timely manner. A celeration aim is a line of progress drawn on a chart at a certain angle from the learner's first performance frequency to the frequency aim. The celeration line tells how many days it should take for the student to reach the performance aim. As such it provides an empirical definition of progress. The angle of the celeration line can be set to expectations that derive from group norms, individual histories of learners, and size of the curriculum slice that students are practicing. At Morningside, we've found that expectations matter. Although we have not conducted empirical studies, we, along with other practitioners of Precision Teaching have noticed that establishing contingencies for rate of progress as well as for eventual rate of performance results in faster growth and more rapid completion of a course of study. In other words, when teachers expected rate to multiply by 1.25 in a week (from 60 per minute to 75 per minute), students tended to match that celeration aim. However, when the aim was set higher, for example a doubling of frequency each week is required, and students receive points on their daily report card for speedier rate improvement, overall celeration appeared to improve. This is another question that bench scientists may want to investigate using controlled research (see Chapter 12).

As students practice, they plot their own frequencies and compare their progress to the celeration aim lines. Their comparisons tell them whether they are making sufficient progress or whether they need to ask the teacher or another student for help. Practice is spaced and cumulative in order to maximize its effectiveness. Here's an example. Let's say the task is "read short passages and select the most valid conclusion that can be drawn from reading the passage from a list." In learning channel terms, this would be stated: see passage/select conclusion from list. Before practice begins, each student inspects their performance chart (see Figure 10) to determine how many passages they need to read and conclusions they need to select in three minutes in order to stay on or above their celeration slope. After setting this goal, the student completes one or more three-minute timings until they achieve their frequency aim. "Drawing conclusions" is a type of skill for which performance can be expected to double in about a week with brief daily practice. This represents a celeration of X2 ("times two"). A celeration aim of X2 means that the slope of the celeration line from the student's entering frequency to the frequency aim reflects a doubling in frequency per week.

Practice activities are designed to include more items than the learner can possibly complete during the timing interval. This protocol ensures that the measurement system is sensitive to growth in frequency and doesn't apply a ceiling or limit to the performance frequency that a student could possibly achieve. Because students practice a skill several times a day, multiple versions of practice sheets are created to ensure that students are responding to variations in the tasks rather than memorizing their order. Students complete several timings in one practice session; the number of timings depends upon how many it takes to reach the frequency that keeps them on their X2 celeration slope.

For selected tasks, students who meet their performance aim during a one-minute timing move into an *endurance phase.* Endurance training ensures that students maintain speed and accuracy for longer periods of time. For example, readers who have met aim for reading prose during 1-minute timings may slow down if the timing duration is extended. Because typical reading assignments in textbooks and novels rarely last only 1-minute, the student is given the opportunity to build endurance, engaging in performance for progressively longer-duration timings, from 2 minutes to 20 minutes or more.

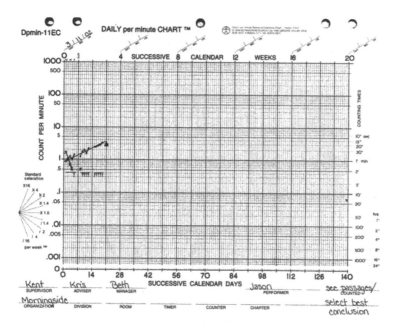

Figure 10. A standard celeration chart showing aim, prescribed celeration line, and frequencies of correct and incorrect performance in selecting conclusions that can be drawn from reading passages (i.e., see passage and set of conclusions/select best conclusion.

A Word About Mastery

These practice sessions blend the timing, charting, frequency-building, and celeration-building aspects of Precision Teaching and the mastery learning, cooperative learning, and peer coaching features of the Personalized System of Instruction (Keller, 1968; Keller & Sherman, 1974; Sherman, Ruskin, & Semb 1982). The goals of our mix of mastery learning procedures are to assure that students permanently retain the skills they are taught; can perform them for extended periods; can perform them in a distracting situation; and can easily apply them, both to new learning requirements and in the course of living life.

111

In traditional classrooms where mastery is not the end goal, *time to learn* objectives or a module or topic *is held constant*, and, as a result, *quality of learning varies*. Both time and quality cannot be held constant. For example, teacher may devote 1-2 weeks for a unit on learning how to predict an outcome during reading, or a two-week unit on fractions, or a month to learn persuasive writing. At the end of the time frame, the teacher may test her students' competency, or a project may serve as evidence of progress. Progress will vary from the most to least "capable" learners. In contrast, in a mastery-based instructional system such as Morningside's, *quality of learning is held constant* and *time is allowed to vary*. Learners who need extra mathetical lessons receive them. Learners may gradually peel away from a mathetics lesson to engage in fluency practice, while others remain for more. If students fall too far behind the homogeneous group, they may move to a slower or lower instructional group. During practice, learners need different amounts of timings or different numbers of days to reach daily and ultimate frequency aims; so be it.

Individuals familiar with the mastery learning literature know that some of the data supporting its superiority were contaminated by pre-test to post-test drop out rates. That is, struggling learners were more likely than able learners to drop out. Those who remained produced exciting learning gains. We don't experience that same problem at Morningside Academy where our dropout rates are very low. Instead of allowing students to experience program failure and give up, we do continuous regrouping to ensure that students are placed appropriately and receive adequate support. Like the ideal mastery learning approaches were intended to encourage, the variable is time to completion of a course of study. Even in the applications of the Morningside Model at our partner schools and agencies, dropouts are rarely, if ever, a function of students' academic progress.

Application

Morningside teachers arrange classroom contingencies to build fluent tool and component skills that are readily calibrated and which can stand alone during an instructional or practice regimen. But authentic problems don't come in these readily calibrated forms, and masterful performance on tools and components doesn't automatically result in their strategic application to solve problems. Thus, application is the third activity that occurs in a daily class session at Morningside. After instruction and practice, students apply the skills they have learned in the context of compound-composite tasks such as games, simulations, and real-world applications. Effective application activities adduce a recombination of key component elements already in the learner's repertoire, to achieve a certain outcome or effect. Application activities may require the teacher to prompt the necessary recombination of elements, or the activity itself may produce automatic recombinations of elements.

Most classroom schedules today are driven by activities, not instruction. The activities are made up of challenging compounds to stimulate creative principle applying and problem solving (strategy learning). Project-based learning is currently in vogue from late elementary school through college. It assumes that students can perform all the component elements and that the composite, compound tasks will produce the appropriate contingency adduction. Most project-based learning arrangements are an "upside down" approach to curriculum planning: the compound comes first out of which both compound and elemental learning are expected. Some educators think projects are inherently interesting and stimulating and believe these anticipated motivational features outweigh component skill weaknesses. The assumption is that, if the task is sufficiently interesting, learners will employ a battery of skills to figure it out. In the end, some learners do, and some learners don't. While we agree that meaningful projects are important educational endeavors, we design Dewey's progressive, real-world applications by introducing compounds later in a "right side up" sequence of instruction that teaches from elements to compounds.

We design at least two kinds of application activities. The first kind requires the student to engage in a previously learned performance in a new context. Students may read a newspaper and discuss the articles with their peers after reading essays in their controlled reading program and engaging in teacher-directed discussions. They may also write a letter to the editor of the newspaper about a particular article after learning and practicing the basic rubrics of writing a persuasive essay. Students may apply a comprehension skill such as drawing conclusions and predicting an outcome while they read a novel or textbook chapter.

The second kind of application activity we design requires new combinations of previously learned elements. More advanced operations in arithmetic, such as long multiplication or division of numbers, are recombinations of previously taught addition, subtraction, and multiplication elements. More advanced forms of sentences and compositions are recombinations of elements learned separately during previous writing instruction. More advanced field sports are recombinations of many previously learned motor activities and chains. The compound called debating combines elements such as argumentation rules, oratory style, Robert's Rules of Order, and quick refutation. The elements in all of these activities can be separately taught; the compound can be taught as an application activity that can recruit the necessary elements. In both cases, application does not describe the opportunity; rather it describes successful extensions and recombinations to fit the requirements of the existing contingencies.

Both kinds of application activities promote generativity and contingency adduction, helping to evolve creative thinkers and problem solvers over time. Applying generic reasoning and self-regulation skills also greatly improves application performance. Students can learn to monitor their own performance and apply reasoning skills to recruit appropriate component elements they have already mastered. We will discuss our evolving delayed prompting procedures, thinking aloud problem solving procedures, and methods of data collection to guarantee these outcomes in the next chapter.

Perhaps the greatest challenge is not in designing application activities, but rather in designing assessment strategies to evaluate the quality of the application. During application, learners produce answers that vary even though a number of variations can be correct. When one and only one answer is correct, one can reliably "grade" the response. When answers can vary, it is more difficult to achieve reliability of scoring. At Morningside, we are developing rubrics by which the quality of an answer can be assessed in a way that has reasonable reliability. But like our counterparts in the public schools, we are finding assessment of authentic outcomes and project-based activities to be challenging.

CHAPTER 6
COMPREHENSION, CRITICAL THINKING, AND
SELF-REGULATION

Morningside has wrestled with the problem of guaranteeing that skills taught in isolation truly become an integral part of the everyday activity of the learner. Two methods that we are evolving are designed to bridge typical behavioral skill instruction and useful, real-world application in the spirit of progressive education and John Dewey. When we discuss our procedures with developmental psychologists, constructivist educators, and others outside of the field of applied behavior analysis, we have found them receptive. This is in part a response to our respect for many of their philosophies, methods, and materials. Many of these colleagues maintain active dialogue with us in our joint effort to find and develop technologies of teaching from basic skills to inquiry and project-based learning.

Delayed Prompting

An important reading application activity in our curriculum involves strategically applying comprehension skills during reading. The context includes a group of students who are taking turns reading a selection aloud. At certain points a teacher stops the reading and engages in "think aloud" monologues that model applications of comprehension skills that the students have previously learned in isolation. For example, the teacher may pause the group reading at various points to make a prediction about what will happen next or what a character will do, or she may make a connection between the plot or a character and her own life experience. After two or three teacher think-alouds that apply a comprehension skill, the teacher uses a *delayed prompting* method to assess and prompt student application of the skill.

Delayed prompting is a question and answer volley between teacher and student. First, the teacher calls on an individual student and provides the opportunity to answer a question (apply a comprehension skill) without prompts. The teacher listens to the answer and decides whether or not it meets criterion. If it does not, the teacher then provides a minimal prompt to adduce the application, and asks the student to answer again. If the answer still does not meet criterion, then the teacher provides a more intensive prompt and asks the student to answer again. If the answer still does not meet criterion, the teacher models a criterion answer and the student then imitates it in his own words.

Here's an example of delayed prompting during group reading:

- (Group members have been taking turns reading aloud. Teacher stops students periodically and begins a delayed prompting interview with a comprehension skill he has *not* taught.)

- Teacher (stops reader): "Hmm, at this point while I'm reading along, I might be thinking about the author's point of view and biases. What seems to be the author's point of view here?" He pauses, then calls on Suzie (not the reader).

- Suzie: "The author seems angry about something."

- Teacher: "What is she angry about, what point of view is she expressing?" (Light prompt)

- Suzie: "Something about how the animals are being treated."

- Teacher: "Why don't you reread that last paragraph to yourself and tell me more about the author's point of view." (Light prompt)

- Suzie (reads to herself, then says): "Oh, about how people in Colorado entertain themselves by organizing cockfighting contests between chickens, and betting on the winner."

- Teacher: "How do you know the author is angry?" (Light prompt)

- Suzie: "She just sounds it."

- Teacher: "Oh, and I see many words that tell me she is angry. One is in the first line. She says cockfighting is cruel. Can you tell me more words that show that her point of view is against cock fighting?" (Heavy prompt)

- Suzie: "Oh, like terrible, and inhumane, and selfish."

- Teacher: "Good. Now tell me about the author's point of view in that paragraph and back up your answer with details." (Light prompt)

- Suzie gives a criterion answer.

- (Several months of practice go by)

- Suzie contributes to group reading discussion by commenting upon the author's viewpoint, backing up her statements with details.

After each question, the teacher pauses to give the student time to think about the question and construct an answer. These volleys, which last for about a minute total, continue until the student provides an answer that meets criterion. Thus the student stays engaged with the teacher until she is successful, no matter how many volleys occur between them. The teacher provides increasing support until the student is successful. The relevant data to collect is the number and kind of teacher prompts that were provided, not the accuracy of the student's response, since all students stay engaged with the teacher until they are successful. We are evolving a data collection method to evaluate teachers' use of prompts, the overall effectiveness of prompts, and the degree of effectiveness of various kinds of prompts across comprehension skills.

The short-term goal of delayed prompting is to guarantee that learners will a) provide answers that meet specified criteria to teachers' requests to employ a set of comprehension skills; and b) self-initiate the use of appropriate comprehension skills and employ them effectively without prompts during group story reading. The long-term goal is that learners will self-initiate the use of appropriate comprehension skills and employ them effectively without prompts during silent reading of passages. Thus, mastery of skill application occurs over successive stories, factual passages, and opinion pieces, not within a given passage.

Notice that the delayed prompting method is a reverse of mathetics' demonstrate, prompt, and release steps. In delayed prompting the teacher tests, then prompts, then finally models until student performance meets criterion. Initial data with our middle schoolers show that six months of daily delayed prompting of comprehension skill application exercises may have produced average reading comprehension gains of 19.5 percentile points or 2.6 grade levels on the *Iowa Test of Basic Skills*. Typically *Iowa* test data of middle schoolers at Morningside after six months show about 1.5 years of growth.[12] Delayed prompting could be used to promote any application, for example in social studies and science classes or in any other situation in which the learner is to apply a skill that has been instructed previously in isolation.

Critical Thinking

Morningside directly instructs and monitors improvement in strategic thinking, reasoning, and self-monitoring skills. Strategic thinking is the glue that allows students to employ component skills and strategies in productive problem solving. Typically, problems provide opportunities for learners to combine known associations, algorithms, and concepts in ways that may not be dictated by an existing formula or that may yield more than one answer. Morningside's instructional and practice strategies build tool and component skills that are needed to solve problems. In addition, most of our students need direct and explicit instruction in "process" or "integrative" repertoires—methods that help them recruit relevant knowledge and skills to solve a particular problem. At Morningside we have found that these strategic thinking skills, characteristic of everyday intellectual activity, are not automatic by-products of learning tool and component skills.

The importance of problem solving has made it the topic of considerable research and the focus of many classrooms around the world. Teachers devise interesting, authentic problems that are appropriate to the age, grade, or entry-level skills of learners who are encouraged to think about them. In fact, some classrooms take pride in their problem-

---

[12] Of course, these are not the kind of data that can rule out other factors responsible for the increase in achievement. Only rigorously controlled research experiments can rule out alternative explanations.

based classrooms. Teachers themselves engage in productive problem solving in a variety of ways and related to a variety of classroom and academic problems.

There are a number of reasons why traditional efforts to promote creative thinking and problem solving have not been wholly effective. First, watching someone else solve a problem does not reliably teach the process. Second, in routine practice, problem solving behavior is private behavior that other learners can't observe. Third, cooperative problem solving often reinforces already-existing problem solving repertoires of some students in the group, but doesn't enhance the skills in others, even though everyone may come away from the group believing they have "solved the problem."

We directly teach a productive type of thinking and problem solving through reasoning. It involves a dance between a speaker and a listener that resides in the same body. Self, as speaker, constantly provides practical, supplementary verbal stimulation to self as listener. The speaker constructs responses during a series of private volleys, prompts, and probes of her own behavior. At Morningside, we view the failure to self-monitor and reason during problem solving as a failure of instruction rather than as a failure of the learner. This perspective has provided a challenge to develop instructional strategies that turn learners into productive thinkers and problem solvers.

Thinking Aloud Problem Solving

To develop these strategies and to provide students with a set of self-monitoring, reasoning, and problem solving strategies, Morningside turned to an approach developed by Arthur Whimbey and Jack Lockhead in the 1970s (Whimbey & Lockhead, 1999). They developed Thinking Aloud Problem Solving (TAPS) to improve analytical reasoning skills of college students. Perhaps the most impressive evidence of its effectiveness comes from its use at Xavier University in a four-week pre-college summer program for entering students. The program, *Stress On Analytical Reasoning (SOAR)*, was replicated over several summers at this predominantly African-American college and produced stunning results. Students who completed the program were two times as likely as non-participants to pass science and math classes. Participants gained 2.5 grade levels on the *Nelson-Denny Reading Test* and an average of 120 points on the *Scholastic Achievement Test*.

Since that time, in a variety of settings with learners of varying ability, the SOAR/TAPS technology has produced improvements in a number of areas, including reading comprehension, particularly with inferential questions; vocabulary acquisition; writing and editing skills; math performance, particularly the ability to articulate how an answer was derived; direction-following and understanding assignments; and performance on standardized achievement and aptitude tests.

Dr. Arthur Whimbey and his colleagues, in *Blueprint for Educational Change* (Whimbey, Johnson, Williams, & Linden, 1993), cite five categories of common errors in problem solving: inaccurate reading, inaccurate thinking, weak problem analysis, lack of perseverance, and failure to think aloud. Table 18 provides examples within each category.

Dr. Joanne Robbins, associate director and principal of Morningside Academy, has adapted Whimbey and Lockhead's methodology for younger children and has proceduralized the instructional regimen. Her adaptation forms the basis of the TAPS work we do at Morningside Academy. A more detailed analysis and description of TAPS comprises Chapter 7.

Table 18. Common Problem Solving Errors (Whimbey et al., 1993)

Inaccurate Reading	<ul><li>Does not stop and check for understanding</li><li>Reads too rapidly</li><li>Skips key facts and words</li><li>Does not re-read difficult sections</li></ul>
Inaccurate Thinking	<ul><li>Inconsistent interpretations</li><li>Chooses procedures at random</li><li>Inaccurately visualizes the problem</li><li>Draws a conclusion too quickly</li></ul>
Weak Problem Analysis	<ul><li>Makes a bad choice about where to begin with the problem</li><li>Moves in too large or random steps</li><li>Doesn't access prior knowledge and experience</li><li>Does not paraphrase</li><li>Does not construct a graphic representation</li></ul>
Lack of Perseverance	<ul><li>Makes little attempt to solve the problem through reasoning</li><li>Gives the problem only superficial consideration</li><li>Solves the problem mechanically</li><li>Gives up and guesses</li></ul>
Failure to Think Aloud	<ul><li>Does not vocalize thinking in sufficient detail</li><li>Performs computations or draws conclusions without explaining why to oneself</li></ul>

While there is mounting evidence about the effectiveness of TAPS in instilling the process or integrative repertoires necessary to recruit tool and component skills to solve problems, it is not clear why it is effective. Teasing out the variables that account for its effectiveness is an ideal topic for controlled research (see Chapter 12).

Self-Direction and Independence

When visitors drop by Morningside Academy, they might very well get the best lesson in the Morningside Model of Generative Instruction from one of the students. This is because Morningside teachers constantly and intentionally strive to make the instructional protocols and decision-making process transparent to parents and students. They encourage students to take charge of their own learning. Teachers discuss instructional and placement decisions with students. They know when programs are working and when they are not. With Precision Teaching, students learn important goal setting, self-monitoring, self-management, organizational, and cooperative learning skills. Students chart their own timings and begin to set their own celeration aims—sometimes much more ambitious ones than the teacher would have set for them. Students manage their own practice and recommend program modifications.

Students also learn self-management and self-determination through freedom to take their own performance breaks and still meet their expected goals, skip lessons when they can demonstrate mastery, move through the curriculum at their own pace, select their own arrangement of tasks to accomplish in a class period, choose their own free time activities, and give themselves report card points, among other opportunities.

All of this is just what teachers are looking for. There is, one might say, a hidden curriculum that doesn't stay hidden for long. Students are at Morningside to acquire knowledge and learn a set of skills, but they also are there to learn how they did it and how they do it best.

CHAPTER 7
PROBLEM SOLVING, REASONING, AND
ANALYTICAL THINKING WITHIN THE
MORNINGSIDE MODEL

Joanne K. Robbins[13]

The analysis of learning outcomes (Tiemann & Markle, 1983, 1990) combined with instruction founded on sound design principles (Markle, 1990) empowers educators to teach the most complex of cognitive skills. Morningside Academy faculty and designers fully believe and work toward the radical notion that intelligence can be taught. Today's Morningside classroom integrates instruction in effective problem solving, reasoning, and analytical thinking, drawing primarily from the investigation of problem solving processes pioneered by Drs. Benjamin S. Bloom (1950), John Dewey (1933), B.F. Skinner (1957, 1969), Richard W. Samson (1975), who credits Albert Upton's methods of 1933, Art Whimbey (1975), Art Whimbey and Jack Lockhead (1991), Susan Markle and Sally Droege (1980), Marcia Heiman and Joshua Slomianko (1988), Joanne Robbins, Joe Layng, and Prentiss Jackson (1995), and Joanne Robbins (1996).

That students should be skilled problem solvers, reasoners, and analytical thinkers is not under dispute. Most educators agree that teaching students to be good thinkers is important and that rote memorization, although having value, must augment, not replace, the ability to problem solve on one's own. However, there is no consensus about how to teach these skills. A longitudinal study conducted at McMaster

---

[13] Dr. Robbins is the Associate Director and Principal of Morningside Academy.

126

University (Woods, 1998) on approaches to teaching problem solving provided evidence that three approaches often used to teach problem solving don't work. To summarize from the McMaster report [italicized text not in original]:

> Ineffective approach #1: *Give students open-ended problems to solve.* This approach is ineffective because the students get little feedback about the process steps, they tend to reinforce bad habits, they do not know what processes they should be using and they resort to trying to collect sample solutions and match past memorized sample solutions to new problem situations.
>
> Ineffective approach # 2: *Show students how you solve problems by working many problems on the board and handing out many sample solutions.* This, we now see, is ineffective because teachers know too much. Teachers demonstrate "exercise solving." Teachers do not make mistakes; they do not struggle to figure out what the problem really is. They work forwards, not backwards from the goal. They do not demonstrate the "problem solving" process; they demonstrate the "exercise solving" process. If they did demonstrate "problem solving" with all its mistakes and trials, the students would brand the teacher as incompetent. We know; we tried!
>
> Ineffective approach #3: *Have students solve problems on the board; Different students use different approaches to solving problems; what works for one won't work for others.* When we used this method as a research tool, the students reported "we learned nothing to help us solve problems by watching Jim, Sue, and Brad solve those problems!

Many teachers will recognize these approaches. Whereas the goal of creating good problem solvers seems to be shared by nearly everyone, there is less clarity about how to achieve the goal. However, there are some promising approaches, one of which is the McMaster Problem Solving Program. This program improves the problem solving, reasoning, and analytical thinking skills of students. Almost all successful approaches share two characteristics: 1) they are relatively unknown and 2) they were developed for high school age students and above. This chapter will summarize some of the effective strategies that can work, and how the author and her colleagues at Morningside Academy and elsewhere have designed effective programs to teach these vital skills to children much younger than college students.

At any given time, the Morningside Academy population may include students whose tested intelligence is below average and students whose tested intelligence is above average. Experts in the field of teaching problem solving and thinking skills have remarked that certain procedures are reserved for students of particular intellectual or academic ability level. One of the limitations of thinking aloud, which many problem solving approaches advocate, is its "difficult[y] for students, especially for younger ones and some of those considered to be academically at risk" (Beyer, 1997, p. 128). Experts in the field of gifted education are cautious as well. Dr. Anthony LeStorti's recent paper (2000) highlights the position that developing thinking skills for gifted children offers special challenges. Morningside Academy faculty members employ the same instructional and motivational procedures to develop problem solving, reasoning, and thinking skills with all students. We have found that explicit research-based instruction leads to eager, inquisitive, and successful learners.

Professional development seminars for faculty who study the Morningside Model of Generative Instruction (Johnson & Layng, 1992, 1994) teach instructors to identify which teaching technology to "pull out of the tool box." Teachers learn to utilize the analysis of learning channels (Haughton, 1972, 1980) and then measure these learning channels and monitor progress with Precision Teaching. They also learn how to carefully analyze the type of learning

(Tieman & Markle, 1983, 1990) and sequence as needed using direct instruction (Englemann & Carnine, 1982), mathetics (Gilbert, 1962), instructional systems design (Markle, 1990), or delayed prompting (Ellson, 1969; Johnson, 2001; Touchette, 1971). Recently, the seminars have also included teaching and promoting effective problem solving, reasoning, and thinking instruction in a progressive education format.

Definitions

Skinner's analysis of problem solving proposes that "two stages are easily identified in a typical problem" (1969, p. 133). He describes the first stage of problem solving as, "the situation for which a response has not previously been reinforced, and the second stage as the process of solution, that is, "the behavior which brings about the change is the problem solving and the response to it is the solution." Whereas the stages may be easily identified, Skinner also points out the ubiquitous nature of problem solving. "Since there is probably no behavioral process which is not relevant to the solving of some problem, an exhaustive analysis of techniques would coincide with an analysis of behavior as a whole" (p. 133).

Accordingly, numerous definitions of problem solving have been proposed. For my purposes in this chapter, the *problem solving* to which I refer is defined as a behavioral sequence, in a situation of defined parameters, which leads to a defined outcome as stated by an instructor, within a text, or by the learner. This type of problem solving is to be distinguished from analytical thinking. *Analytical thinking* is a similar behavioral sequence, but involves a further element of inquiry and situations with less well-defined parameters and outcomes. Analytical thinking is necessary when an ambiguous situation requires the learner to identify or create a problem to solve. *Reasoning*, an essential element of both problem solving and analytical thinking, involves the manipulation of verbal stimuli to restrict response alternatives in accord with a problem's outcome. That is, when the environment requires a learner to produce verbal stimuli that sequentially and systematically make one pattern of behavior more likely than another in order to meet a contingency requirement, reasoning is defined. This process is akin to what Skinner (1969) described as an "inspection of reinforcement contingencies" such that behavior can be described that meets contingency requirements without direct contingency shaping or rules. Procedures have been developed that train learners in reasoning and in the inspection of the requirements for reinforcement in most problem solving situations.

The Role of Verbal Behavior

As noted above, one key element of the approach is the production of verbal stimuli that guides the learner through the problem solving sequence, or as more commonly described, the use of thinking or talking aloud during the reasoning process. Although often approached as a skill to be learned, most young children spontaneously engage in these processes when learning something new. Berk (1994), who studied the private speech of children in natural settings, reports that private speech "either described or served to direct a child's actions, consistent with the assumption that self-guidance is the central function of private speech." (p. 80). Summarizing her research with a variety of populations including longitudinal studies of elementary students in a university lab school, low-income Appalachian children, and youth diagnosed with attention-deficit hyperactivity disorder, Berk concludes that, "the evidence as a whole indicates that private speech is a problem solving tool universally available to children who grow up in rich socially interactive environments" (pp. 82–83). When comparing the Appalachian students in her research to Lawrence Kohlberg's observations of middle-class children,

Berk reports an increasing frequency of self-talk for the middle-class children between the ages of four and six which then decelerates during elementary school and becomes inaudible muttering. By age ten, the Appalachian children's private speech is audible 40 percent of the time compared to the middle-class students who spoke aloud only 7 percent of the time. Additional variables occasioning private speech include the task demands, that is, the level of challenge and the social context of the environment.

We, at Morningside, value Berk's suggestion: "The most profitable intervention lies not in viewing private speech as a skill to be trained but rather in creating conditions that help children use private speech effectively" (p. 83). We rely on Skinner's (1953, 1957, 1969) analysis to plan and best arrange such conditions.

One's own description of a performance while it is occurring may have a history of success for any number of reasons. The beginner cook may find himself repeating the written quantity of ingredients aloud while measuring and leveling off the ingredients. "In constructing external stimuli to supplement or replace private changes in his behavior, a man automatically prepares for the transmission of what he has learned. His verbal constructions become public property, as his private discriminations could not. What he says in describing his own successful behavior can be changed into useful instruction" (Skinner, 1969, p. 139). This same instruction when the speaker is his own listener while problem solving may even, at times, be considered a source of automatic reinforcement "where the speaker generates stimuli to supplement other behavior already in his repertoire" (p. 442).

That is, the behavior generated by the supplemental verbal behavior may be recognized (discriminated) as providing a solution or a step toward the solution, thus, maintaining the problem solver's behavior (Catania, 1975; Goldiamond, 1976). The question raised is, how do we teach the effective use of supplementary verbal behavior as part of the problem solving process?

Skinner succinctly points out the dilemma of the radical behaviorist who designs instruction that employs sound instructional design principles. "It is because programmed instruction eliminates much problem solving that some objections have been raised against it. The programmer solves the learner's problems for him. How does he do so? What must the instructional designer do if he is either to study or to teach problem solving?" (p. 135).

To design an ideal system of instruction (see Markle & Tiemann, 1967), a culture of thinking is first established as inspired by Project Zero (Tishman, Perkins, & Jay, 1995), a Harvard-based research group that investigates problem solving, creativity, and thinking. The text, *The Thinking Classroom: Learning and Teaching in a Culture of Thinking* (Tishman, Perkins, & Jay, 1995)—an outgrowth of Project Zero—introduces "six dimensions of a culture of thinking: (1) a language of thinking (2) thinking dispositions (3) mental management (4) the strategic spirit (5) higher order knowledge and (6) transfer" (p. 2). Although seemingly contradictory, a direct instruction approach, which provides the teacher with a script and the students with opportunities to respond chorally (as a function of errorless learning; Markle, 1990) and with faultless communication (Englemann & Carnine, 1982) was selected as the most efficient way to create such a culture. Thus, the establishment of a highly independent student repertoire, analytical reasoning, is established using a highly structured teacher-dependent lesson. This program is called "TAPS for Teachers" (Robbins, 1996). TAPS is the acronym derived from Whimbey and Lockhead's (1991) paired problem solving, described as Think Aloud

Paired Problem Solving." The scripted instruction, TAPS for Teachers (1996) replaces Whimbey's "think-aloud" with "talk-aloud."

But why talk aloud? In everyday practice, "we speak aloud to ourselves upon occasion—for example, when the audible response improves intraverbal chaining. In the solution of a difficult problem, mathematical or otherwise, we resort to overt responses, vocal or written. For the same reason, such covert behavior as counting money or adding figures is likely to become overt in the presence of distracting stimuli" (Skinner, 1957, p. 436). When learners are acquiring a new skill we may even see a greater tendency to disruption by distracting stimuli. Indeed, test designers often include textual "distracters" to separate good problem solvers from bad. Accordingly, to ensure that the problem solving process is occurring, that effective verbal behavior is produced, and that the behavior will not be easily interrupted, a talk aloud protocol is utilized.

The three strategic systems that we employ in teaching basic skills (reading, writing, mathematics) and content courses (e.g., history, culture and geography) are TAPS, Thinking Aloud Problem Solving; Suchman Inquiry (Suchman, 1966); and FTS, Fluent Thinking Skills (Robbins, Layng, & Jackson, 1995). Scripted lessons are part of both the TAPS for Teachers and FTS programs. The strategies are taught using abstract or content-free materials and then are transferred to the content classes and everyday life experiences. With these strategies in full swing; a Morningside classroom is noisy, happy, analytical, reflective, and filled with determination.

TAPS for Teachers

This program is built on the foundation of the speaker as own listener. The power of this dialogue between the speaker and listener in one body, that is speaker-as-listener, forms the basis of both the TAPS for Teachers and Fluent Thinking Skills lessons. As a learner engages in challenging material or studies textbook material or reviews notes from a lecture, the Morningside student engages in a process of self-questioning and checking. Figure 11 below lists qualities of the speaker and listener, which develop outside of the problem solving, thinking and reasoning classroom and are regarded as tool skills that facilitate the composite events. Dr. Kent Johnson, founding director of Morningside Academy, designed this skill profile.

The scripted TAPS lessons introduce the qualities of the two repertoires to be constructed, that of the speaker, called the *Problem Solver,* and that of the listener, called the *Active Listener.* Students are paired, with each alternating as speaker and listener as problems are solved. Whimbey and Lockhead's (1991) system, first called Cognitive Process Instruction, extended Bloom's (1950) work, with the critical difference from Bloom's approach being the partnered dialogue. Without an Active Listener, the Problem Solver's verbalizations or construction of external stimuli goes without reinforcement and support. TAPS for Teachers teaches students and teachers the qualities needed for each role. Students in the program study the qualities exemplified by each member of this volley. These qualities or repertoires, though based on Whimbey and Lockhead's original profile, have been expanded to include other qualities as a result of errors commonly made by students during developmental testing of the program (after Layng, Stikeleather, & Twyman, 2004; Markle, 1967).

Student name		Teacher:_____ Classroom:_____ Start Date:_____ End Date:_____	
		Communication Skills	objectives
		Listening	19
		Asking questions	20
		Different proportions of telling, listening, and asking	21
		GROUP DISCUSSION SKILLS	
		Addressing the group	22
		Handing off	23
		Taking turns	24
		Brainstorming skills	25

Figure 11. TAPS speaker/listener skill profile.

To ensure that students are able to respond along all of the dimensions of a good *Problem Solver* and *Active Listener*, the class works through several phases. The first several days of instruction, the teacher leads the class through the scripted instruction. The culture of thinking is built with students making signs and posters using the vocabulary words presented in their workbooks. A cartooning exercise (see Figure 12) engages the student to sketch what they witnessed during demonstrations of each of the attributes of the Problem Solver and Active Listener. The instructor models a full set of examples and nonexamples of the qualities of the two repertoires with student volunteers rotating as partner to the instructor. Students identify both the good qualities and poor qualities of both speaker and listener repertoires. These repertoires include specific domain-free problem attack strategies (see Markle & Droege, 1980) as well as specific prompting strategies employed by the Active Listener to assist the Problem Solver. As the students move to paired problem solving, the high level of activity required of both members of the pair creates a noisy, productive environment.

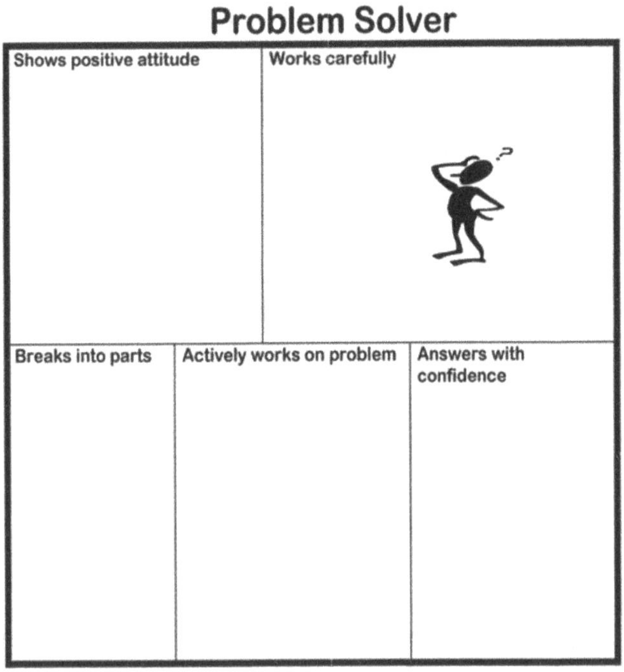

Problem Solver

Shows positive attitude	Works carefully	
Breaks into parts	Actively works on problem	Answers with confidence

Figure 12. TAPS cartooning. Copyright © 2004 K. Melroe & J. Robbins.

One problem confronted by younger learners is a lack of a vocabulary of problem solving. As a result, both speaker (Problem Solver) and listener often exhibit a great deal of hesitation, long pauses, repetition, and disconnected comments. As Skinner (1957) describes, when a verbal response is required to "fill an embarrassing pause, we cast for a stimulus" (p. 403). A classic example is chatter about the weather. By teaching the TAPS for Teachers vocabulary to the Problem Solver and Active Listener, the students have access to the words or prompts necessary during those moments when a verbal response is required to provide supplemental support in the problem solving process. By providing a culture of thinking in a classroom that is filled with visual examples of the process being taught, the reasoning process can be shaped, and the learners' "casting about" can be recruited to move the process along.

After the two repertoires are established, the reasoning process proceeds as an interaction of the two repertoires occurring within the "same skin"; that is, the student takes on both roles: Problem Solver and Active Listener. The Problem Solver produces a goal directed dialogue, while the Active Listener evaluates the dialogue for its progress in meeting the problem solving goal. The students have learned to listen to themselves, evaluate their own effort, and provide verbal feedback that prompts further action and eliminates alternatives. One often observes an instance of "self-strengthening" described by Skinner (1957), whereby the speaker-as-listener re-reads directions or reads a problem slowly or reads it in parts until the problem solving goal is clearly stated. Sometimes the speaker or Problem Solver is unsure or appears to lack confidence; that is, the learner may emit a weak, hesitant, or incomplete response. The Active Listener, who is the same person as the Problem Solver, may hear the response and add further dialogue that prompts yet other responses, in a process like that described by Palmer (1991) in his behavioral interpretation of remembering. Stated differently, it is at those moments when the Problem Solver's

137

response is weak, perhaps having forgotten a detail, that the same person as listener will be able to recognize the correct response even though there was a hesitation in its production.

The reasoning process may also make use of a series of formal or thematic prompts (see Markle, 1969; Skinner, 1957); reading the text of the problem aloud again may provide an opportunity to inspect the text for the required information. Students are taught to change the emphasis, to stop at particular words that are key to the meaning—sometimes as simple as the word NOT—(a thematic prompt). The process is not unlike what Skinner (1957, p. 406) describes as "hoping that an intraverbal relation will supply needed information."

We constrain the reinforcement system by initially requiring all taught qualities of the Problem Solver and Active Listener to be present while students complete their logic and analytical reasoning exercises. For example, "Have a positive attitude" is one such quality that may be demonstrated by a student saying, "I can do it. I will solve this problem." Teachers continuously reinforce approach behavior in the context of the Morningside Daily Report Card. A student earns learning skills credit for emitting such a response. The Problem Solver and Active Listener repertoires, which are initially rule-governed, become contingency-shaped as the students move through a variety of exercises and then are prompted to "use their TAPS" during basic skills and content class instruction. Students are considered skillful when they can inspect the problem space, describe the requirement that must be met for reinforcement (solution), and produce a self-dialogue (i.e., they reason) which produces the final behavior.

In summary, "Even fragmentary descriptions of contingencies speed the acquisition of effective terminal behavior, help to maintain the behavior over a period of time, and reinstate it when forgotten. Moreover, they generate similar behavior in others not subjected to the contingencies they specify. As a culture evolves, it encourages running comment of this sort and thus prepares its members to solve problems most effectively" (Skinner, 1969, p. 143).

TAPS can also be used to reason through cases of practical deliberation taken from daily life. Dewey described the importance of practicing "practical deliberation" in his book for education majors, *How We Think* (1933). Teachers demonstrate how to apply TAPS to situations, such as the best way among several alternatives to reach a destination within a given time frame. Students are asked to select situations from their own lives for which TAPS might be helpful. Students are encouraged to apply TAPS as they reflect upon things they observe, such as how a back porch they see on the way to school was probably built. In the gradual shift from teacher-directed to student-directed learning, students master learning skills using Thinking Aloud Problem Solving, which weans them from teacher dependency to independent learning. However, identifying and framing the conditions where TAPS can be most useful ultimately requires an additional repertoire: analytical thinking.

Analytical Thinking

As noted earlier, analytical thinking is necessary when an ambiguous situation requires the learner to identify or create a problem to solve. It involves the reasoning process described above, but involves a further element of inquiry, often in situations with less well-defined parameters and outcomes. This skill is required when a learner faces an often ill-defined, more global problem. Here's a typical school situation the student might face when they realize that a test is coming up: "What do I study, and how do I know what is important?" In a work situation, the problem might be a slow down in providing customer assistance or missed opportunities to develop new products. Before one can apply their reasoning skills, it is critical that there is a clear idea of what it is that needs to be reasoned. Though overall content knowledge is important, one's responses to ambiguous situations help describe the differences between someone skilled in a discipline and someone new to it.

Where the problem is not clear, the strategy required is one of inquiry, and to inquire is to question. Questioning combined with reasoning, thus, is the key to analytical thinking. In John Dewey's words (1986, p. 330), "Thinking is inquiry, investigation, turning over, probing or delving into, so as to find something new or to see what is already known in a different light. In short, it is questioning."

Questions in reading comprehension exercises generally are presented following a prose reading. Students are to "test their understanding" of the text with the questions. Unfortunately, this approach is based on a rather passive view of how one learns from text. The question this approach raises is: at what point is the learner to think analytically about the text? If the learner is answering other people's questions, either posed by a teacher or provided at the end of a text, can the learner really be described as engaging in truly analytical thinking? Based upon Markle's (1990) first principle of instructional programming: "the student learns what the student does" (p. 1) the answer is "no." Active responding, the behavioral term for what cognitive psychologists call "meaningful responding" must be verified if we are to ascertain that the activity leads to learning (Markle, 1990). Brethower's (Heimann & Slomianko, 1985, p. 16) observation of successful college students found that they

> Ask questions of new materials, engaging in a covert dialogue with the author or listener, forming hypotheses, reading or listening for confirmation;

Identify the component parts of complex principles
and ideas, breaking down major tasks into smaller units;
Devise informal feedback mechanisms to assess
their own progress in learning; and
Focus on instructional objectives, identifying and
directing their study behaviors to meet course objectives.

Simply reading text cannot be considered either very active or meaningful responding. When questions are posed after text is read, students must often reread the text to find the answers and become engaged in the act of answering, rather than being engaged in an act of discovery or inquiry. Conversely, orienting questions, provided by the text or a teacher, and presented prior to the reading task, may serve a different function. They may tap prior knowledge, facilitate recognizing important passages while reading, and provide a basis for feedback as to whether or not the text is understood (Osman & Hannafin, 1994).

Another system of question-generating instruction is derived from the work of Dale Brethower at the University of Michigan in the 1960s who, in turn, refined the SQ3R (Survey, Question, Read Recite, Review) techniques originally designed by Robinson (1946) and revised by Fox (1962). This "Learning To Learn" system (Heiman & Slomianko, 1985) has resulted in significantly improved grades and retention through graduation and is the only college-level program certified by the U.S. Department of Education as producing such gains. The Learning to Learn (LTL) system has been further refined by Robbins, Layng, and Jackson (1995) into a program known as Fluent Thinking Skills.

Whereas the TAPS procedures prepare students for the final three observations of the four described by Brethower, the first, questioning, must be taught separately and added to the learner's repertoire to produce a true analytical thinker. Teaching students how to question, therefore, has become a central part of the Morningside program. Students learn to question in a variety of contexts and this skill is later combined with the problem solving skills that have been acquired and practiced through our TAPS program.

Several strategies are used to teach questioning. One is based upon the familiar game of 20 questions and is known as the Suchman Inquiry Approach (after Suchman, 1966). After students read or hear a short mystery or puzzling scenario, they generate questions that are answered by the teacher with an answer that is either yes or no. Rudolf Flesch (1951) in "The Art of Clear Thinking" advocates strongly for this exercise: "And that's why, if you're interested in producing ideas, the Greek yes-or-no game is useless, while the game of twenty questions is the ideal model" (p. 112). Critical Thinking Books and Software publish readily available mysteries that can be used to shape up these skills; one series is called "A Case of Red Herrings." To shape up better question generating, the students collect all questions generated and rate them after the solution has been attained. This exercise helps students apply a questioning strategy in a non-textual environment.

The primary strategy for teaching analytical thinking, however, is the Fluent Thinking Skills program. The program consists of a series of systematically designed instructional sequences and practice exercises that teach different types of questioning, and then provides considerable guided practice in their application. Once the questioning skill is firmly in place, students are taught to apply it to textual material they are to learn.

Students are asked to first generate questions to textual material without fully reading it. They base their questions on the headings, sub-headings, initial sentences in a paragraph, captions, and so on. Once the questions are posed, the students are asked to answer them prior to reading the text.

One of the critical features of the Fluent Thinking Skills program is that each student must find each discrepancy between the answer to the self-posed question and the response request specified within the text (or lecture material). Figure 13 shows the work of a middle school student using the Fluent Thinking Skills approach with a science text. Each learner creates and identifies a unique discrepancy based upon individual experience. This requirement of self-questioning and finding the discrepancy between what the learner initially calls the "Best Guess" and what the text provides as the answer is labeled "Not match," and defines what the learner needs to learn. It is the comparison of what the learner knows prior to reading and after reading that defines the discrepancy. The reading-to-answer-questions approach targets exactly that which is missing from the learner's repertoire. Students are encouraged to apply their TAPS skills to first answer their question, and then to resolve the discrepancy.

Once students have mastered this process, other strategies are added such as using charts and graphs to see relationships in the subject being studied, finding sameness in related concepts, and extending relations to areas outside of what is being studied, among others. What has emerged is a general rule: we learn through discrepancies (cf. Donahoe & Palmer, 1994), and we extend what we know through samenesses (cf. Skinner, 1957).

J

poor conductors of heat and electricity. Also, they are usually brittle, not ductile or malleable. It should also be noted that there are fewer nonmetals than metals. Only about twenty elements are distinctly nonmetallic. How many of them can you name?

Q — Describe how the placement in the table works.

PLACEMENT IN THE TABLE

(A — It is when something is being placed
BEST GUESS — in like the table of contents.
Look again at the periodic table on pages 130–131. *It is like putting it in the categories*
Notice the zig-zag line on the right-hand side of the
table. Metals are to the left of this line. Nonmetals are *Not Match*
to the right.

① They were talking about graph,
Keep in mind that the properties of the elements in a *and was talking about categories*
given row are not alike. At the far left, elements are dis- *② They were talking about*
tinctly metals. At the far right, they are nonmetals. *elements and I thought it was*
Thus, there is a shift in properties from metals to non- *table of contents.*
metals as you move across a row from left to right.

A result of the shift in properties is that some elements—especially certain ones near the zig-zag line—have some metallic and some nonmetallic properties. Elements like this are called **metalloids** (MET-'l-oids). Boron (B), germanium (Ge), silicon (Si), and arsenic (As) are good examples. These elements are semiconductors—that is, they conduct electricity, but not as well as metals. This property makes them useful in many electrical devices, such as transistors.

Figure 13. Student questioning sample.

CHAPTER 8
TEACHING READING, WRITING, AND MATHEMATICS

Morningside Foundations program teachers devote 90 minutes each day to teaching primary academic foundations—reading, writing, and mathematics. The three levels of teaching that we described in Chapter 5—instruction, practice and application—lead to mastery of the instructional objectives in each domain. The curriculum within each domain is divided into three hierarchical levels: basic tool skills, intermediate component skills, and composite or compound skills. Table 19 shows the typical time allocated to each level within each domain.

Table 19. Time Allocation in Morningside Instructional Blocks for Reading, Writing, and Mathematics

Time	Reading	Mathematics	Writing
30 Minutes	Tool Skill Fluency	Tool Skill Fluency	Tool Skill Fluency
	word mechanics, phonological coding, decoding, oral reading	reading numbers, writing numbers, math facts, identifying place value, solving simple equations, factoring, multiples	handwriting, transcription & dictation in writing and typing; spelling, word processing

continued...

30 Minutes	Component Skills Fluency	Component Skills Fluency	Component Skills Fluency
	background information, vocabulary, retelling, comprehension skills	computation skills, math concepts, comprehending quantitative statements	sentence combining (sentence structure, grammar, mechanics)
	generic integrative skills (e.g., identifying problems, TAPS, identifying relevant components)	generic integrative skills (e.g., identifying problems, TAPS, identifying relevant components)	text reconstruction (organization and sequence)

choosing words precisely to convey meanings

Instruction and practice in writing paragraphs and essays and reports in different writing genres. |

continued...

30 Minutes	Compound Repertoires	Compound Repertoires	Compound Repertoires
	Strategic application of background knowledge, vocabulary, and comprehension skills during group reading and discussion Strategic application of generic integrative skills	Strategic application of computation skills, math concepts, and quantitative relations to quantitative, project-based investigations and inquiries. Strategic application of generic integrative skills	Strategic application of sentence writing, sequencing, and word choice skills to writing paragraphs, compositions, & reports in different genres Strategic application of generic integrative skills (e.g., identifying problems, TAPS, identifying relevant components)

Three Generic Hierarchical Curriculum Levels

As we have discussed, basic tool skills are the fundamental units of performance, those minimal response sets (Alessi, 1987) that underpin virtually all of the instructional objectives in each foundation domain. Think of a tool skill as the hub of a wheel with many spokes, each spoke representing a component skill in a domain, the wheel itself representing a domain. Fluent tool skills facilitate the learning and fluency of each component, which in turn facilitate the learning and mastery of the compound repertoires, those most authentic indicators of competence in everyday life. For example in reading, phonics and other word identification skills are tools for mastering vocabulary and comprehension skills. To comprehend a story or essay, the learner must be able to read the words it contains. To master long division, a learner must know her math facts. A learner cannot write good sentences unless she can produce letters and correctly spelled words.

The relation between intermediate component skills and compound repertoires shows a dependency similar to the one that holds between tool skills and intermediate component skills. Authentic, real-world compound repertoires are composed of intermediate component skills. When we call someone an excellent reader, we mean that they demonstrate an authentic, real-world approach to reading—a compound repertoire. They are strategic and engaged when they read. Such strategic, engaged reading requires the application of many component reading skills, including background knowledge and vocabulary inherent in what is being read, and application of many comprehension skills, such as making predictions, drawing conclusions, and making connections between what they are reading and other aspects of their lives or other material they have read. Real-world quantitative reasoning and problem solving—the authentic, compound mathematical repertoire—requires application of many intermediate component skills, including computation, quantitative concepts, and understanding of verbal/quantitative statements. Excellent writers demonstrate a compound repertoire that requires application of many component skills, such as sentence writing, organization and sequencing of sentences and paragraphs, and selecting words to have the best effect upon a reader.

This structural account presents an incomplete picture of the relations between and among the three levels of curriculum in each domain. Other parts make up the whole besides the skills defined in each level of the domain. Other repertoires are required to bridge and integrate between tool skills and component skills and between component skills and compound repertoires.

At Morningside, we have found that the integration of tool skills and component skills is fairly straight-forward; high frequencies of tool skills make it likely that they will occur as required during the acquisition of component skills; at most a few prompts may be necessary.

The integration of component skills and compound repertoires is more complex. In addition to fluent component skills, other repertoires must be learned and applied during the application process. These include some organizational and sequential behaviors, and the overall Thinking Aloud Problem Solving (TAPS) repertoire. Other problem solving skills are also required, including learning to see a problem or opportunity when one occurs; exploring, selecting, and specifying components in one's repertoire that are relevant; and summarizing one's place in the application performance at many points throughout that process. These *integrative repertoires* must be instructed and practiced until fluent, and then systematically applied when appropriate. The application phase of instruction is the place where component skills and integrative repertoires come together. For example, during strategic, engaged reading, a word, phrase or other unit of meaning may prompt the reader to converse with himself about the relation between what is being read and previous readings and life experiences. The reader could engage in the TAPS protocol to explore these past events, select ones to compare and contrast in specific detail, organize and summarize the similarities and differences, and later report to listeners and readers. The reactivity of readers and listeners will serve as natural reinforcers to make certain reports more and less likely in the future.

Reading
   Tool Skills. Table 20 presents the specific reading tool skills, component skills and compound repertoires that we teach. Teachers spend approximately 30 minutes each day instructing and arranging the practice of phonics, word identification skills, and expressive oral reading to fluency aims. Direct Instruction and Precision Teaching are used to teach these skills and make them automatic. The programs we use range from *Headsprout Early Reading* and *Read Well* at the beginning level, to decoding programs for struggling readers (for example, Maloney's *Teach Your Children to Read Well*, Engelmann's *Corrective Reading–Decoding*), to skill-based bridges to basal readers such as Dr. Anita Archer's *REWARDS* and *REWARDS Plus*. Teachers apply DI techniques in what we call "boardwork" to teach word identification skills, which include letter sounds, letter sound combinations, word parts, word sounding out procedures, and word-part emphasis ("accenting"). Students monitor their progress and request interventions with Standard Celeration Charts for see/say sounds, words, and/or prose fluency. When students have difficulty learning word identification skills, teachers break them down further and teach deficient auditory sensory

behaviors (*Phonological Coding*; Haughton, 1999), and/or deficient visual sensory behaviors (*Rapid Automatic Naming* [*RAN*]; Haughton 2003). When students have mastered these tool skills, more time is spent teaching levels 2 and 3, and learners advance to standard basal reading programs such as *Scott Foresman 2002* and *Open Court 2002* for grades 2–6, and Holt's *Elements of Literature, 2005* for middle and high school. (See Table 1 for details of recommended programs.)

Component Skills. Teachers spend approximately 30 minutes each day instructing and arranging practice of component skills. Prior to each selection that the class will be reading, teachers use mathetics to "pre-teach" prerequisite facts, concepts, and principles ("background knowledge") that will maximize initial comprehension of upcoming reading selections. In an informal arrangement called "Activating Prior Knowledge," teachers ask students to contribute their own background knowledge to the background knowledge the teacher presents.

In the middle 30 minutes of a reading block teachers also use mathetics to instruct students in vocabulary relevant to an upcoming reading selection. We have developed nine mathetical formats for teaching vocabulary: (1) modeling, (2) synonyms, (3) definitions, (4) advanced definitions, (5) meaning in context, (6) paraphrasing definitions, (7) matching, (8) assertions using vocabulary: Yes, No and Why, and (9) sentence completion. Teachers "pre-teach" vocabulary by selecting words and phrases from upcoming selections that they anticipate will need instruction and practice, examining the nine mathetical formats, and selecting one or more that would be appropriate for each word. Students practice vocabulary using a Precision Teaching technology called SAFMEDS: "Say All Fast, Minute Each Day, Shuffled." SAFMEDS is a flash card fluency technology developed by Dr. Steve Graff. The technology includes software for producing

SAFMEDS cards and an instruction manual for writing cards that promote fluency, illustrated with lots of examples and nonexamples of flash cards (Graff & Lindsley, 2002). Vocabulary is taught and practiced a few times each week or more, as needed, to accelerate progress on celeration charts.

Teachers also teach comprehension skills each day. Typical lists of comprehension skills include 20 or more, such as author's point of view and bias, stating the main idea, predicting an outcome, drawing a conclusion, making a connection, summarizing a section, and so on. Morningside has developed a six-step mathetical format for teaching comprehension skills. After instruction, learners may practice applying the skills to short passages in rapid succession to build fluency.

Students also learn generic problem solving skills such as TAPS, and other integrative repertoires during the component skills portion of the reading block.

Compound Repertoires. Teachers spend the final 30 minutes of each reading block developing compound repertoires while learners read a selection from their reading program as a group. The selections gradually increase in length and complexity of word attack, vocabulary, and comprehension as students advance in grade levels. Selections eventually include novels and nonfiction books, and content textbooks in Morningside's Middle School laboratory. Morningside has a specific protocol for monitoring the decoding performance of students during group selection reading, adapted from Engelmann's *Reading Mastery VI Teacher's Guide* (SRA, 1984). Group selection reading occurs most days.

At significant points during group selection reading, teachers model application of both integrative repertoires and comprehension skills during group selection reading. Teachers use the delayed prompting technology described in chapter 6 to help students practice applying both integrative repertoires and comprehension skills.

After students finish a reading selection, they retell it. We use Dr. Anita Archer's *REWARDS Plus* methods to teach students how to extract details from a selection, and we extend her design by including broader formats for more formal story-telling and information monologues. Teachers model good retelling, and ask students to practice retelling to their reading group. Students receive praise and corrective feedback for their retelling performance from the teacher and their peers. Morningside students work in pairs to develop checklists, and listen and score each other's retelling performances using the checklists. Free/say retelling is monitored on Standard Celeration Charts. Students practice retelling for a couple of days after finishing a selection, or more as needed to accelerate progress on celeration charts.

Writing

Tool Skills. Teachers spend approximately 30 minutes each day instructing and arranging practice of the basic tools skills of writing. These include handwriting; keyboarding skills; transcription, or copying from text just below their instructional reading level; taking dictation from spoken passages; spelling; and word processing on a computer. See/write and type letters, then words, then passages; hear/write and type letters, then words, then passages; hear/write and type spelling words are all monitored on celeration charts. For very early learners, tools skills such as paper position, pencil gripping, and writing basic shapes are also practiced and monitored on celeration charts.

Component Skills. Teachers spend approximately 30 minutes each day instructing and arranging practice of two sets of component skills: sentence combining and Text Reconstruction.

Arthur Whimbey and Myra Linden are pioneers in the development of sentence combining technology (Linden & Whimbey, 1990; Whimbey, Johnson, Williams, & Linden, 1993). In sentence combining exercises learners put two or more sentences together. Teachers teach a sequence of sentence combining patterns, each of which focuses upon a particular grammatical convention. For example, to teach conjunctions, teachers use mathetical lessons to teach the discrimination between and, but, for, and so in the context of combining sentences. Here's an example:

- Sentence 1: My neighbor said she wanted to go to Europe in the worst way.
- Sentence 2: I let her take my kids.

Students choose the correct punctuation and the correct connecting word. In this case, they would choose a comma and the connecting word "so." They then combine the sentences to achieve this compound sentence: "My neighbor said she wanted to go to Europe in the worst way, so I let her take my kids."

All the rules of grammar and mechanics are taught in this way, including the most complicated arrangements of dependent clauses and use of gerunds as sentence subjects. During instruction students first imitate patterns for combining simple sentences into more complex sentences. During practice, students practice a series of patterns, first in isolation, then in a cumulative mix. Morningside learners monitor and improve their sentence combining skills with celeration charts.

Dozens of studies over 30 years show that with at least 20 hours of practice, sentence combining improves grammar and usage skills, increases the complexity of sentences, improves punctuation skills, improves proofreading skills, increases reading levels, and even increases foreign language learning and the quality of compositions. Studies have demonstrated these effects with a variety of learners from fourth graders through college students. In dramatic demonstrations of contingency adduction, two studies compared instruction in a range of composition genres to instruction in sentence combining alone without genre focus. They found that the sentence combining students wrote better compositions! (See O'Hare, 1973, with 7th graders; Daiker, Kerek & Morenberg, 1979, with college freshmen.) The most recent survey of sentence combining published by the National Council of Teachers of English concludes, ". . . no other single teaching approach has ever consistently been shown to have a beneficial effect on syntactic maturity and writing quality" (Linden & Whimbey, 1990, pp. 23–24).

Whimbey has recently expanded upon sentence combining in a technology he calls Prototype Construction (Whimbey, 2002). The method uses kernel subject-verb-object sentences to teach the general case of sentence writing. Prototype Construction exercises in sentence combining, sentence rearranging, subtracting from sentences, and expanding sentences teach all of the conventions of English grammar, usage, and mechanics.

We appeal to Whimbey and Linden again for our other core intermediate component skill curriculum: Text Reconstruction. Text Reconstruction (TRC) teaches the organization and sequencing skills critical to a compound repertoire of writing (Linden & Whimbey, 1990, Whimbey, Johnson, Williams, & Linden, 1993). During TRC exercises, learners order jumbled sentences into paragraphs, and jumbled paragraphs into essays or stories. If alternative sequences can be justified, teachers lead students to compare their arrangements and discuss the differences. TAPS and its variant "Compare and Discuss" may also be used during practice.

Once sentences and paragraphs are ordered, learners copy the text. Students monitor their progress with celeration charts.

Linden links TRC's heritage to Benjamin Franklin, who worked in his brother's printing shop. His brother was widely recognized for his superior printing; very well-known writers of his time would use his print shop. Franklin would take their manuscripts and cut them up into sentences, put the strips in a box, shake the box, and then reorder and copy the sentences. In an advanced variation on TRC, he would write down only key words from author's sentences, order the set, and attempt to recall the exact wording of the full sentences during the copying phase. He said, "This was to teach me method in the arrangement of thoughts" (Linden & Wimbey, 1990, p. 39), and claimed he owed his writing prowess to this practice.

The ordering contingency inherent in TRC requires the learner to carefully inspect the text. This detailed inspection and copying may produce finer discriminations, thus improving reading fluency, spelling, punctuation, English conventions, and even reasoning skills and mastery of facts and concepts. In fact Linden has written an American History text in TRC jumbled sentences! TRC also involves all four language arts skills: reading, talking, listening, writing, thus increasing its multiplicative power as a component skill.

Both sentence combining and text reconstruction may be applied to the learner's own writing process. Each sentence of first draft compositions can be written to the margin. The composition can then become a personal sentence combining exercise, and a text reconstruction exercise to improve the organizational and sequential aspects of the composition.

Compound Repertoires. Teachers spend approximately 30 minutes each day instructing in and arranging practice of writing paragraphs and essays and reports in different writing genres. In the primary grades we use Dr. Siegfried

Engelmann's Direct Instruction *Expressive Writing* I and II programs. In grades 4 through adult learning we use Dr. Anita Archer's (2002) *An Instructional Model for Teaching Written Composition.*

Archer's writing program teaches the critical attributes of seven writing genres, including descriptive paragraphs and reports, factual paragraphs and reports, persuasive writing, business letter writing, and narrative writing. Students encounter both examples and nonexamples of good writing in each genre, and use writing rubrics to judge their quality. For example, the rubric for a descriptive paragraph asks learners to rate the quality of a descriptive paragraph in the following manner:

1.   0 1 2 3 4 Does the first sentence tell what is being described?
2.   0 1 2 3 4 Do the other sentences tell more about what is being described?
3.   0 1 2 3 4 Are descriptive words used?
4.   0 1 2 3 4 Are the sentences written in logical order?
5.   0 1 2 3 4 Does the paragraph paint a clear and accurate picture of what is being described?
6.   0 1 2 3 4 Is the description easy for the reader to understand?

Using a mathetical design, a teacher models use of the rubric, leads students to help her use the rubric to judge the quality of other paragraphs, and, when accurate, tests the learner's independent use of the rubric to judge additional paragraphs. Students practice writing descriptive paragraphs and use the rubric to improve their work. Students apply the rubrics to each other's writing and share their writing with the class.

As in reading, during the final 30 minutes spent developing compound repertoires, teachers model and students practice strategic application of component skills. These range from sentence writing, sequencing, and word choice skills to writing paragraphs, compositions, and reports in different genres. Students also practice applying sentence combining and text reconstruction to their own writing. Teachers model strategic application of other problem solving repertoires during writing, including TAPS, so that students learn to examine their own writing, question how they've written, and ultimately improve their written product.

Mathematics

Tool Skills. Teachers spend approximately 30 minutes each day instructing and arranging practice of reading numbers, writing numbers, math facts, identifying place value, solving simple equations, factoring, and giving multiples of a number. Morningside Press publishes materials for building all of the math tool skills.

Component Skills. Teachers spend approximately 30 minutes each day instructing and arranging practice of computation skills, math concepts, and comprehending quantitative statements. Generic integrative repertoires are also taught during the middle 30 minutes, including identifying faulty quantitative reasoning, TAPS, and identifying relevant components needed to solve math problems. Morningside recommends Saxon Mathematics and Engelmann's Connecting Math Concepts series to teach math component skills.

Compound Repertoires. Teachers spend approximately 30 minutes each day modeling and arranging practice of strategic application of computation skills, math concepts, and quantitative relations. Teachers also model strategic application of generic integrative repertoires. They use the delayed prompting technology described in chapter 6 to help students practice applying both integrative repertoires and component mathematics skills. They also lead learners in quantitative, project-based investigations and inquiries. Saxon Math includes math investigations.

Conclusion

In a constantly evolving mode, each year the protocols for teaching reading, writing and math are revised based upon new instructional research and new published programs. All revisions conform to the Morningside Model of Generative Instruction. The process follows Markle's system of instruction. Each revision also analyzes curriculum into the three hierarchical levels, according to the Tiemann and Markle learning outcomes model, complete with learning channels. Curricula are carefully sequenced to maximize mastery, fluency, celeration, and contingency adduction. The revised curricula are implemented according to the 3 phases of teaching characteristic of the Model and in the instructional blocks described above.

Each year's Summer School Institute provides the opportunity for Morningside staff to share curriculum and interventions that have been learner-verified during the previous year and to show how these new approaches are integrated into the existing menu of options in each curricular area.

CHAPTER 9
CLASSROOM MANAGEMENT WITH A DAILY
REPORT CARD

Morningside classrooms are busy, high-energy classrooms. In a typical Morningside classroom, three different groups might be engaged in three different activities. One group may be in a lesson with the teacher. Another group may be practicing in pairs, and the third group may be engaged in TAPS. Even though the teacher is conducting a lesson, he or she must also ensure that other students are on-task. Morningside's commitment to learning and, in many cases, to making up for lost time means that students need to be academically engaged throughout a class period. There's no time to waste and no time for disruptive behavior. All of this means that teachers need to establish workable classroom routines, and students need to develop a battery of skills that support their learning.

The Daily Report Card has evolved since Morningside's inception (Johnson, 2004) to become the first line of prevention in a Morningside teacher's classroom management toolbox. At the beginning of each day, students receive a daily report card on which is listed their classes and expectations for the day (see Figure 14). Students earn points for demonstrating four categories of skills: academic, learning, organization, and citizenship (see Table 20).

Behavioral expectations are stated clearly and posted on the wall. At the beginning of the school year and when new students enter the program, teachers model and prompt the behaviors that are expected. Teachers set aims in each category each day. One point is earned for either achieving an outcome or making an improvement toward a final outcome.

The aim for the class is set at 90% of the total number of points that could be earned for the set of tasks and activities that make up the agenda for the class period.

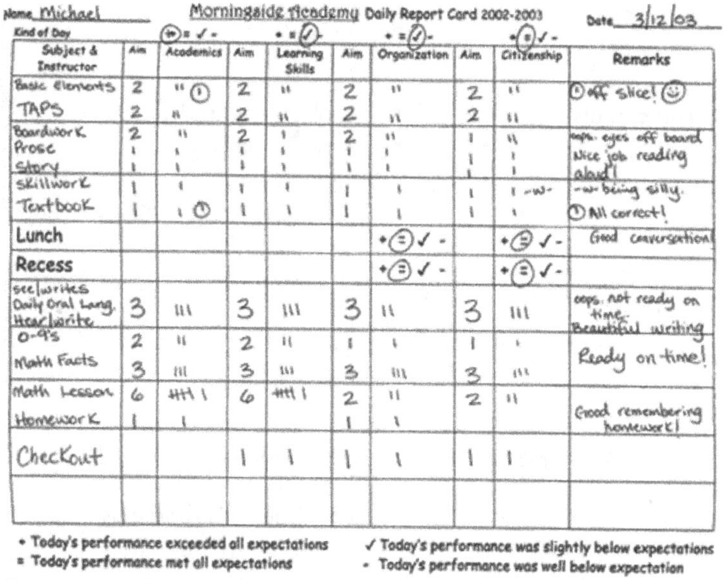

Name Michael — Morningside Academy Daily Report Card 2002-2003 — Date 3/12/03

Kind of Day: Academics (+) = ✓ - ; Learning Skills + = (✓) - ; Organization + = (✓) - ; Citizenship + (=) ✓ -

Subject & Instructor	Aim	Academics	Aim	Learning Skills	Aim	Organization	Aim	Citizenship	Remarks
Basic Elements TAPS	2 2	II (1) II	2 2	II II	2 2	II II	2 2	II II	(1) off slice! ☺
Boardwork Prose Story	2 1 1	II I I	2 1 1	I I I	2 1 1	II I I	1 1 1	II I I	oops. eyes off board Nice job reading aloud!
Skillwork Textbook	1 1	I I (1)	1 1	I I	1 1	I I	1 1	I -w- I	-w- being silly. (1) All correct!
Lunch						+ (=) ✓ -		+ (=) ✓ -	Good conversation!
Recess						+ (=) ✓ -		+ (=) ✓ -	
see/writes Daily Oral Lang. Hear/write	3	III	3	III	3	II	3	III	oops. not ready on time. Beautiful writing
0-9's Math Facts	2 3	II III	2 3	II III	1 3	I III	1 3	I III	Ready on time!
Math Lesson Homework	6 1	~~IIII~~ I I	6	~~IIII~~ I	2 1	II I	2	II	Good remembering homework!
Checkout			1	I	1	I	1	I	

+ Today's performance exceeded all expectations
= Today's performance met all expectations
✓ Today's performance was slightly below expectations
- Today's performance was well below expectation

Figure 14. A completed Morningside Academy daily report card.

Teachers distribute points in each category throughout each class period. Students can earn "bonus points" for extraordinary performance. At the end of the day, students meet individually with their final class period teacher, who totals their points and circles the "Kind Of Day" they achieved in each category: "A +" for exceeding the day's total aim; an "=" for meeting the "A" level standard reflected in the day's total aim; a "✓" for missing the total aim by one or two points, or a "-" (minus) for earning 3 or more points less than the total aim (carefully inspect Figure 14).

Table 20. Examples of Expectations in Each Daily Report Card
Category

Academic Skills	<ul><li>Meets or exceeds performance aims</li><li>Shows adduction or generativity</li></ul>
Learning Skills	<ul><li>Looks like a student</li><li>Answers on signal</li><li>Follows along</li><li>Follows directions the first time</li></ul>
Organization Skills	<ul><li>Is on time</li><li>Has necessary materials</li><li>Keeps work area neat</li><li>Charts in pencil</li></ul>
Citizenship	<ul><li>Uses appropriate language</li><li>Respects others' space</li><li>Uses voice appropriately</li><li>Uses body appropriately</li><li>Respects physical property</li></ul>

The teacher and student also discuss their academic progress and comportment. The teacher writes summary comments, and students take the report cards to their families who in some instances sign and return them. Family conferences are scheduled for students who earn more than 3 consecutive minuses in a category or more than 3 minuses in a week.

The Daily Report Card operates at several levels. First, it controls teacher behavior, serving as a visible reminder to observe and respond to student behavior. Second, it reminds students of their daily goals, prompts appropriate performance, and provides concrete evidence of progress. Third, it operates as a token economy in which points earn items and activities of value to the learner.

Ideally, Morningside strives for a situation in which learning and meeting important educational goals serve as powerful reinforcers for students. However, many of the students who come to Morningside are not responsive to these more abstract consequences. About a third of the students at Morningside use their Daily Report Card points to choose from a menu of desirable options, such as access to computer games during recess, or extra TV or telephone time that evening. For them, the points serve as conditioned reinforcers, and the menu establishes a proper balance between deprivation and satiation with respect to individual menu items.

Both the points and the back-up rewards are consequences that are unrelated to the behaviors that earn them. Extra telephone time at night bears no natural relation to solving new math problems and reading more fluently. For students who have experienced failure in education, positive natural consequences may be few and far between. In such cases an arbitrary reinforcement system provides a much-needed bridge to help the learner come in contact with the naturally reinforcing consequences of intellectual success and making progress in academic pursuit. A danger lies in maintaining an arbitrary reinforcement system beyond its usefulness, however. Ultimately our goal is to bring intellectual pursuit under its own naturally reinforcing consequences.

Skinner's colleague Dr. Charles Ferster (1967, 1972, 1974) wrote extensively about the distinction between arbitrary and natural reinforcement and argued for more natural reinforcement in applied behavior analysis. Arbitrary reinforcement is applied to behavior defined by the controller, he said, while natural reinforcement selects behavior from the current repertoire of the learner. Whereas arbitrary reinforcement produces short-term benefits usually maintained only in the presence of the teacher, natural reinforcement is long-term, maintained by multiple environments. Arbitrary reinforcement produces a limited number of behaviors, under a limited number of conditions, i.e., those specified by the teacher. Natural reinforcement, on the other hand, is not dependent upon a teacher or certain circumstances and can thus produce a wide variety of behaviors under a wide variety of conditions, each time it occurs.

Problems associated with arbitrary reinforcement are more benign when curriculum and instruction are geared to teaching students generalized imitative repertoires in reading, writing and mathematics. Arbitrary reinforcement is much more problematic when the curriculum shifts to content study and project-based learning. In his book for teachers, *How We Think*, Dewey (1933) cogently expressed the problem of "satisfying the teacher instead of the problem," and making "the child a student of the teacher's peculiarities rather than the subjects that he is supposed to study" (pp. 160-161). He warned that schooling misses the point when the student's "chief concern is to accommodate himself to what the teacher expects of him, rather than devote himself energetically to the problem of the subject matter. 'Is this right?' comes to mean 'Will this answer or this process satisfy the teacher?'—instead of meaning 'Does it satisfy the inherent conditions of the problem?'" (p. 161).

To address these problems in our middle school program we are developing a multi-leveled daily progress report system that fades from a teacher-defined daily point system to student documentation of accomplishment, self-evaluation, and teacher reactions, as students move from foundations skills learning to content learning and project-based learning.

Each year, Morningside's routine procedures for encouraging self-management prove ineffective with a very few students. In such cases, a more thorough analysis of the learner's history and current contingencies results in specialized programs that assist students in achieving classroom behaviors that recruit adequate reinforcement from those around them and stabilize their academic progress.

CHAPTER 10
TECHNOLOGY TRANSFER:
DEVELOPING PARTNERSHIPS,
TRAINING, AND COACHING

Morningside designs and implements instruction for students who need to learn basic reading, writing, and arithmetic skills and for those who are trying to catch up in academic content areas like social studies and science, but these are not its only important clientele. Morningside also helps the teachers who will implement these programs. They, too, require carefully designed training programs and rubrics to guide their performance with their students. Morningside Teachers' Academy applies the same exacting standards to its teacher preparation programs as it does to its reading, mathematics, and writing programs.

This chapter emphasizes the implementation that occurs at external schools and agencies that contract for services with Morningside. When an external agency applies to be a partner school, it is almost always because they are impressed with the outstanding results Morningside has achieved with students. Often, administrators from the agency will have visited Morningside and observed the assessment protocol, the curriculum, and the pedagogical techniques that constitute the program, but they are rarely aware of the teacher training that has established the very polished routines they witness nor are they aware of the underlying philosophic and theoretical assumptions that undergird the program. They want results. Still, to become a Morningside partner school, external agencies must agree to the extensive training and school reform that we've come to know are necessary for a school to implement the program with procedural reliability and, thus, to obtain the results we promise. These contingencies are described in great detail during the contractual negotiations. Agencies are encouraged to bring a core group of teachers and other personnel to the annual Summer School Institute, and many do. During the Institute, participants not only hear about the Morningside Model, they see it in action and participate in applying it.

Morningside's approach to technology transfer and teacher training has evolved over the years and continues to evolve. It is informed by an extensive literature on staff development. Although Morningside Teachers' Academy attempts to be flexible and to develop individual plans with schools and agencies that request its services, some very specific parameters define the conditions under which Morningside will offer its technologies for transfer. First, school leaders must agree to support the program by encouraging faculty and staff to complete training and implement program procedures in their classrooms. Leaders must also recruit the participation and support of teachers and other staff to implement the program. Leaders are encouraged to adopt positive support strategies with their staff.

Over the years, Morningside has worked with certified teachers, teachers who do not have formal certification, paraprofessionals, parents, principals, school psychologists and school counselors, and any number of other school and agency staff or affiliates who have taken on the job of teaching children. Some already have well-honed content and pedagogical knowledge. Others have virtually none. Still, all of them have one unifying goal: they want to or have been asked to teach basic skills and content to learners.

We have worked with teachers and other staff in urban schools, rural schools, public schools, and private schools. We have worked with people who represent institutions that serve primarily low-income students and those who represent wealthy citizens. A full range of races and ethnicities have been part of the student and teacher corps with whom we've worked.

Currently, the training and technology transfer process mirrors the teaching process that we use with our students. Training occurs first with teachers who join the staff at the Morningside Academy laboratory school. It also is offered to teachers and graduate students who participate in the Summer School Institute. Last, it is offered to faculty at partner schools and agencies. There are five elements to Morningside's current process: orientation to the Morningside model; explicit instruction in curriculum; assessment; pedagogy; role-playing with peers, coached application in classrooms, and institutionalization of the programs into the school or agency.

Decisions about how and when to emphasize each of several elements is based on an analysis of the agency and its teaching and administrative staff.

Orientation to the Morningside Model

Morningside Teachers' Academy launches programs in the context of its strong social justice philosophy. Morningside administrative officers believe that schools and agencies have a social and moral obligation to provide access and opportunity to all learners. They believe that education is fundamental to human rights and human choice and communicate this belief to the schools and agencies with whom they work. Morningside administrative officers are drawn to schools and agencies whose students have been disadvantaged in educational opportunities, and they recognize the role of good educational programs in reversing historical racial and ethnic discrimination in this and other countries. Most important, Morningside administrative officers and trainers adopt an attitude of optimism about the possibilities for schools and agencies to reverse historic trends in student performance; they communicate this optimism to the teachers and administrators with whom they work.

When the consultants from Morningside begin their work with teachers and other school professionals, they do so with a goal of creating independent thinkers and problem solvers. For this reason, teachers are provided with an orientation to the Morningside approach. At first, theoretical components are introduced, and understanding of and conversance with the behavioral and progressive education components of the program is shaped over time. Some key elements of the Morningside Model that are presented during orientation include the emphasis on research-based, learner-verified techniques, the role of active responding in the success of the model, the importance of and the rationale for homogeneous grouping, the use of in-class coaching to firm up teachers' skills, the involvement of many people in addition to the teacher in the teaching process, an introduction to principles of content analysis and instructional design, Morningside's multi-level system of assessment, and behavioral and progressive education philosophy.

Research-Based, Learner-Verified Techniques

Most important at the beginning of the partnership is the introduction of the Morningside emphasis on research-based, learner-verified outcomes. Morningside consultants present outcome data from the laboratory school in Seattle and from projects in schools and agencies. Teachers and administrators in the school review the current performance of their learners and set goals about the kind of performance they desire. Morningside's emphasis on continuous monitoring of student performance proves to be the greatest challenges for some teachers, schools, and agencies; consequently, the challenge for trainers is to communicate the critical contribution of continuous performance monitoring to student progress.

Active Responding

During initial work with teachers and external partners, Morningside consultants emphasize the nature of the interactive role of teacher and learner in the Morningside Model of Generative Instruction. Teachers' modes of interaction with their learners have evolved over time, sometimes thoughtfully, sometimes automatically, and these personal styles have become comfortable to them. The high-energy classrooms that characterize the Morningside model may be quite orthogonal to the styles teachers currently use.

Homogeneous Grouping

Morningside Academy groups students homogeneously, an approach that counters current practice in many schools. Morningside trainers work with teachers, schools, and agencies to understand the purpose of homogeneous grouping and to find other ways to achieve the important goals that heterogeneous groupings grew up to facilitate. Some teachers, particularly those whose children have experienced discriminatory practice in schools, are reasonably fearful that homogeneous grouping is code language for tracking and leaving children behind. When teachers hear about the ease with which students are able to move from group to group within the year, based on their progress, and the aggressive goal setting Morningside employs for all learners, they are somewhat comforted. However, true understanding and acceptance of homogeneous grouping occurs when teachers begin to implement the program, recognize placement errors, work together to move students to groups that are more appropriate to their current level, and watch the fluid movement of students from group to group.

Teacher Autonomy

Morningside Academy opens classroom doors and limits teacher autonomy. In some schools and agencies, policy requires administrators to observe teachers as few as two times a year. The Morningside Model is much more intrusive in the lives of teachers. Morningside trainers and coaches will be in classrooms much more frequently, will ask supervisors to increase their observation of teachers during program implementation, and will sometimes ask teachers to videotape classroom performance. Many teachers welcome the support and feedback that accompanies the introduction of the model, but others actively or passively resist it. This means that Morningside trainers and coaches spent a great deal of time building positive relations with teachers and shaping them to accept more and more intrusive feedback in their classrooms. Coaches attempt to accommodate to each teacher's preference for style of interaction and feedback. One school administrator reported that he appreciated that Morningside consultants "get their hands dirty." He reported that many people come to his program and *tell* people what to do. He appreciated that Morningside staff *show* people what to do and *help* them do it. Still, the practice changes a longstanding culture in many schools and provides a challenge to successful program implementation.

Involving All Classroom Teachers and Aides

Morningside attempts to marshal all the resources that are available in a school or agency to achieve good outcomes for learners. This means that traditional roles of teachers, teacher aides, and other support staff may be threatened. Classroom aides participate in training alongside certified teachers, and many prove to be equally capable of implementing Morningside programs. In some schools, parents and other volunteers join the teaching staff so that class size can be reduced. Supervisory and administrative staff are expected to develop expertise on Morningside programs and protocols so that responsibility for coaching teachers can shift, over time, from Morningside staff to local staff. Some teachers are selected by Morningside staff and agency leaders to serve as peer mentors to other teachers in the school. Supervisors and peer mentors hone their coaching skills by working alongside Morningside coaches.

Principles of Content Analysis and Instructional Design

Teachers also are introduced to principles of content analysis and instructional design. When an agency adopts the Morningside Model, teachers and other school personnel receive an overview of the content analysis that underpins the programs teachers will be asked to implement. While many of the teachers that participate in Morningside training already have some or considerable knowledge of the content area they will be implementing, they may have used curricular material that are based on a very different content analysis than Morningside has adopted. Particularly in reading, mathematics, and writing, teachers receive an overview of the content area. For example, in reading, teachers are instructed in the 10 dimensions of reading and learn how Morningside combines commercial programs with its own technological overlays to provide learner-verified instruction.

During early implementation at most sites, fairly structured and scripted curricular materials serve as models for teachers to begin to understand design elements. Some teachers resist the scripted lessons for a variety of reasons. Some have developed philosophic objections to structured lessons, often because they view them as too mechanistic. Others find the procedures diametrically opposed to their own current practices.

Morningside's Multi-Level System of Assessment

Morningside staff engage teachers and administrators in schools and agencies in thinking about their assessment programs. Many schools and agencies have depended on yearly standardized, norm-referenced tests to provide evidence of instructional success. Morningside attempts to change the assessment culture by introducing the rationale behind its multi-level system of assessment. Morningside trainers particularly emphasize the role of continuous measurement in achieving the curricular gains for which Morningside is known. The Morningside approach is contrasted with commonly used measurement systems in use in many educational programs.

Behavioral and Progressive Education Philosophy

Behavioral and progressive education philosophy, and the relations between them, are introduced during orientation. We do this to address suspicions that abound in education circles about behavioral approaches to education and to assure teachers that the values of the progressive education movement are embedded in the Morningside approach. Misrepresentations of behavioral approaches and misunderstandings of progressive educational philosophy have spawned classroom practices that, we believe and evidence supports, constrain student growth. As we describe pedagogical protocols and curricular decisions, we reflect on the philosophic, theoretical, and databased underpinnings as a way to reduce resistance and encourage full teacher participation. We also encourage teachers to raise issues with us. As the staff in schools and agencies become more sophisticated in their practical applications of procedures, we include more philosophic and theoretical discussion during training and casual conversation. And as staff become familiar with and learn to question assumptions that underlie assessment, curriculum, and pedagogy, they move closer toward the independence we desire for them.

Explicit Instruction in Assessment, Curriculum, and Pedagogy

Teachers receive explicit instruction in curriculum packages, assessment, and pedagogical techniques.

Assessment

Entry-Level Assessment. Many schools and agencies routinely administer standardized, norm-referenced instruments at the beginning and end of the year that are required by state or agency policy. Although Morningside encourages administrators to submit to the testing as near to the beginning of the available fall window and as near to the end of the available spring window, Morningside is not otherwise involved in this testing phase. However, Morningside's entry-level test battery includes additional standardized, norm-referenced tests or subtests that are particularly sensitive to student growth, program-specific pretests, and CBM tests. Morningside works with the school or agency leadership to identify a core group of individuals who will conduct entering level assessment and then trains this assessment team in the assessment protocol. Morningside consultants also assist school or agency administrators develop a plan to test all students. Administrators also work together with assessment team members to develop a data tracking system that will provide evidence of student growth from beginning to end of the year.

At the beginning of the process, Morningside staff review students' test scores and recommend placement. For example, in one agency that has contracted for a reading program, students could be placed in one of seven reading levels based on entry test scores. Morningside also shares the decision tree it uses to make placements. So, for example, placement in reading is based on students' performance on a word attack test, a sight word test, a silent reading fluency test, comprehension measures, and oral reading passage fluency. As the process continues, assessment team members recommend placement based on the student's scores and the decision tree and submit these recommendations to Morningside staff or confirm or revise the placement. The goal is for the assessment team to achieve reliability in placement decisions and take over placement of students, although Morningside staff is always available to discuss difficult cases.

Standard Celeration Charting and Precision Teaching. Because practice and frequency building are such critical components of the Morningside Model, teachers are introduced to Standard Celeration Charting and chart-based decision making early on during training. We begin with a brief explanation of the advantages of the Standard Celeration Chart over other more conventional charting methods, making particular note of the value of the celeration chart in guiding teacher's curricular and pedagogical decisions. By the end of the initial training phase, which may occur over multiple training sessions, participants can

- describe the layout of the daily chart.
- label the daily chart.
- read data from the daily chart.
- enter data on the daily chart.
- teach students to drop points on the chart.
- employ the timings practice chart for daily practice.
- transfer data from the timing practice chart to the daily chart.

As these skills become firm, participants learn to

- plot a celeration line based on prescribed celerations for the learning task and channel.
- place a daily goal box on the practice timings sheet, transferring these skills to students as soon as they have achieved reliability with the teacher's goals.
- assess student performance and make programming decisions based on the assessment.

Curriculum

Typically, teachers are asked to develop expertise in one curricular area and one instructional program at a time. Most often, schools and agencies request assistance in reading.

Morningside adopts and modifies curricular packages that contain elements that coordinate with Morningside technologies. In the most common scenario, teachers develop competence in one curriculum area at a time and with one program at a time. For example, in reading, some teachers may develop expertise on phonological coding (e.g., Elizabeth Haughton's *Phonological Coding*) while others focus on programs that teach decoding of single syllable words (e,g, Michael Maloney's *Teach Your Child To Read Well* or Engelmann's *Corrective Reading* Direct Instruction programs) while still others work first with programs that teach decoding of multiple syllable words (e.g., *REWARDS* or *REWARDS Plus*). In this same school, another group of teachers will learn the features of a literature based basal program (e.g., Scott Foresman *Reading 2002*, SRA/McGraw Hill's *Open Court 2002*, or Holt, Rinehart, and Winston's *Elements of Literature*, 2005.) Teachers develop familiarity with the scope and sequence of the program and are given explicit guidance about program elements that Morningside includes in its adaptation of the program.

Reading is a good example of a content area in which teachers, themselves, have some content learning to do. For example, individuals who will be implementing reading programs may not be fluent in the sounds of letters. They are good readers, but they are—as adult readers—less dependent on phonetic structure for word decoding. Thus, some part of training is devoted to teaching these program elements that teachers will need to know to assist students. Interestingly, teachers often report that their own reading has improved because of the work they're doing with their students.

Teachers also are pointed in the direction of important resource material that can supplement the program they will be implementing. For example, in comprehension skills instruction, teachers often need more examples than are provided in their basal reader or anthology to assess students' knowledge of a skill. Morningside provides resources and teaches teachers how to employ them, in this case, in a loosely woven script during group story reading.

Pedagogy

Teachers learn a variety of pedagogical techniques that are essential to faithful implementation of the Morningside model. The primary emphasis is on five elements: setting expectations and classroom management, instructional protocols, practice protocols, peer tutoring/cooperative learning protocols, and TAPS.

Setting Expectations and Classroom Management. The effectiveness of Morningside's curriculum and instructional protocols is in relation to the teacher's skills in managing the classroom. Agencies that believe they need better classroom management may contract directly for this service and receive intensive classroom management and contingency analysis training. However, the more typical case is one in which teachers learn a basic protocol for setting classroom expectations or they learn to incorporate the Daily Report Card.

In the setting expectations training, teachers learn to make explicit all of their expectations for students at the beginning of a class period or for each program activity. The training session on setting expectations clarifies for teachers why it is important to set clear expectations, to verbalize them daily, and to reward students whose performance conforms to the expectations. This method is contrasted with a commonly used approach in which expectations are not stated until they have been violated. Teachers are encouraged to state expectations each time a new activity begins, keep this instructional episode short and concise, and display expectations in the classroom.

Each activity has corresponding expectations. For example, group response boardwork has the following expectations:

- Answer on signal.
- Keep your eyes on the board.
- Use good posture.
- Sit facing forward.
- Use strong, clear voices.
- Raise your hand if you have a question.

Group story reading has a different set of expectations, though overlaps are noted. Teachers learn to set the following expectations for group story reading:

- Follow along in your book when others are reading (using finger, paper, eraser part of pencil).
- Use a strong, clear voice.
- Read with expression.

- Raise your hand (or thumbs up or mark in your book) when you hear an error.

During peer partner work, there are different expectations. Teachers coach students to

- Follow along with their partner.
- Chart every practice.
- Work the entire time.
- Use six-inch voices.
- Talk only about the task.
- Give your partner feedback.

Teacher expectations vary by teacher and by activity, but a general list that is applied by all teachers results in more reliable performance by students and allows teachers to focus on the content of instruction. Teachers coach students to state the expectations, and even young children learn this skill quite readily. Teachers' creativity is most often seen in the ways in which expectations are displayed in their classrooms. Some of the particularly clever examples are pictorial for use in classrooms where children can't yet read.

Many teachers need to be reminded to reward students who comply with expectations. Trainers suggest minimum levels of teacher praise that should be provided as students comply with expectations. Morningside consultants find that even teachers who are warm and encouraging with their students need gentle reminders to increase their rate of rewarding students for good performance. Teachers that have adopted a tough, military style of working with children find this requirement particularly difficult. During training, teachers roleplay instructional sessions with their colleagues and practice using unobtrusive, individualized, and varied praise statements. Later, Morningside coaches observe teachers in their classrooms and keep track of positive and negative comments.

Instructional Protocols. During the earliest work with teachers, scripted lessons are the mechanism through which teachers implement protocols that are appropriate to different learning outcomes. They apply one protocol for teaching associations, another for teaching sequences, and yet others for concepts and principle application. These scripts are based on the work of Susan Markle and Siegfried Engelmann. However, the long-term goal is for teachers to become less dependent on heavily scripted lessons and to be able to apply appropriate protocols in other classroom learning situations.

Therefore, intermediate training is directed toward freeing teachers from scripts and developing their ability to create their own scripts or to apply the teaching principles appropriately. Underlying these instructional protocols is Tom Gilbert's mathetics model. Teachers learn to model, lead, and test students during initial presentation of new elements or procedures. They also learn the reverse mathetics model that underpins the delayed prompting technique, which is appropriate for use during application of previously learned elements or procedures. Special instruction often is required for teachers to be able to choose effective prompts, to correct errors, and to implement discrimination training

A significant part of the instructional work at Morningside uses a procedure that is known as "boardwork" in which the teacher is at the front of a group of students who are responding on cue to the teacher's instructions. Typically, the teacher is following a script and presenting a lesson. It is in this context that the teacher learns to achieve choral responding through signaling, to incorporate the verify, pace, randomize, and individualize stages that are described in detail in Chapter 5, and to provide error corrections.

The signal is the mechanism that ensures choral responding, and is critical to many of the scripted lessons that teachers will use during instruction. Most teachers who participate in training have not used a signal previously, and many are uncomfortable doing so at first. During training, teachers receive explicit instruction in a five-part signaling protocol, and they try out a variety of signals during roleplays with their colleagues until they find one that works well for them. Teachers also learn how to arrange their room to create an architecture that works well for boardwork.

Practice Protocols. In the Morningside model, students practice in pairs to meet their frequency aims. Although practice sessions are less scripted than instructional lessons, students' progress is a function of the structure of the activity. Teachers receive instruction in how to manage the fluency work. Teachers learn to

- teach students how to use timers to accurately time their partners' practice.
- establish pairs by thinking about social compatibility and by choosing partners who have similar or compatible repertoires.
- establish work folders with practice materials, practice charts, and daily charts.
- ensure that practice materials, timers, and other needed items are available before the practice session begins.
- instruct students in where and how materials will be available and what they should do with them at the end of the practice session.
- instruct students in how to record their partner's performance and progress.
- set expectations for the timing session, including the number of practices that should

occur during the interval and what materials are to be available during the work.

- circulate during the practice session to ensure that students are on task, are listening carefully to their partners, are timing accurately, are providing encouragement to their partners, and are recording performance correctly.

- intervene as needed to ensure that the time is being used productively, to instruct the listener about uncaught errors, to encourage more positive support, and to reward students for meeting expectations.

Cooperative Learning and TAPS. Morningside employs peer pairs not only for practice, but also for cooperative learning and other project-based activities. The TAPS procedure that is discussed extensively in chapter 7 has become the basic cooperative learning protocol at Morningside. Just like in practice sessions, teachers have preparatory work to do to set up a cooperative learning activity. Teachers learn how to

- assign pairs, considering academic performance, social skills, and prior relationships.

- arrange seating to assure close proximity within each pair and some distance between pairs.

- assign a specific activity that pairs will work on during the cooperative learning session and set a time limit.

- set expectations for the cooperative learning activity.

- circulate throughout the room giving feedback to students on the process and product of their work, including their compliance with stated expectations.
- correct errors of fact when not doing so will hamper student learning.
- when all groups are working on a common problem, bring the group back together at the end to share ideas and solutions.

As pedagogical strategies are presented, teachers have the opportunity to role play them in pairs or in small groups with peers. Teachers learn quickly that it's one thing to hear about or even talk about strategies; it's quite another to implement them. During workshops, teachers practice and receive feedback from peers and trainers. They learn not only to perform the requisite skills, but also to evaluate the performance of others using standard rubrics that Morningside trainers have designed.

Coached Application in Classrooms

A fundamental component of the Morningside model is the coaching that teachers receive in their classrooms. As the 1987 meta-analysis by Bennett and the work of Joyce and Showers (1995) suggests, in-classroom coaching is a necessary component of staff development. Teachers may acquire the ability to talk about a new program or a new procedure as a result of training, but they do not acquire the ability to do the work without explicit, contextual practice. Even though roleplaying provides useful practice opportunities and smoothes the transition between hearing about a procedure and doing it in the classroom, very frankly colleagues make pitiful actors! Even when they try to act like students, they fail to accurately represent the pitch and activity level of the classroom or to produce the kinds of errors students will produce. Therefore, Morningside has adopted an intensive coaching routine as part of its technology transfer to partner schools.

Morningside trainers note which individual teachers have completed training on which program elements. They then establish a schedule to observe the teacher's implementation of the procedure in his classroom. During the first coaching episode, the teacher may simply implement a sample lesson that was used during training. However, in subsequent lessons, teachers conduct program elements in the context of the program they are implementing.

Coaches use specially designed coaching forms which specify the specific elements they will watch during the coaching session. First the coach checks to be sure that the teacher is prepared for the lesson. This includes having materials ready, having the classroom appropriately arranged, and setting expectations for the students. Coaches then focus on specific elements of the procedure that the teacher is demonstrating.

Here's an example for an instructional lesson where the teacher's performance on "boardwork" is being assessed. The coach will typically observe the clarity and effectiveness of the teacher's signal or the appropriateness of their stepwise progression through the four stages of verify, pace, randomize, and individualize. Coaches will also observe the teacher's compliance with the scripted lesson, note if the teacher is listening carefully to all students, and observe error correction procedures. Coaches will note if the teacher set expectations for the class, and will record the number of positive and negative statements the teacher makes during the lesson.

Coaches also observe the teacher's implementation of the practice session and their compliance with the Standard

Celeration Charting protocol. They observe teachers instructing students and monitoring cooperative learning and group story reading activities. In each case, the coach's feedback is based on a set of criteria that the teacher and coach have agreed to in advance of the coaching session.

Although there is considerable variation among coaches and each coach makes an effort to adopt a coaching style to the preferences of the individual teacher, the coaching process is relatively intrusive. Coaches typically give feedback and make suggestions to the teacher in real time and may model steps that the teacher has not perfected. They also review teachers' charts and chart-based decisions.

Because this coaching process is out in the open, students also are learning how the procedure is supposed to work, and the most self-assured teachers encourage their students to serve as their coaches during lessons. Students enjoy noting teacher errors, but they also provide encouragement to novice teachers. In classrooms where the teacher and student have a positive and encouraging relationship, students can be enormously helpful to the teacher as she proceeds from halting to fluent implementation.

Following the lesson, the coach will sit with the teacher and answer questions and make suggestions. Once teachers have mastered the basic protocols, coaches turn their attention to the teacher's decision making. They review charts and chart-based decisions. They review the progress on lessons and talk with the teacher about placement concerns.

Sometimes, during coaching and subsequent conversations with teachers, the coach recognizes a performance error that has resulted from a training error. For simple procedural matters, emails and notes to teachers are used to correct misinformation. Sometimes the coach will call all the teachers back together to correct the error. Additional

185

training sessions also are scheduled to answer questions that have arisen.

Institutionalizing the Program in Schools and Agencies

Morningside doesn't want to stay in each partner school forever, so efforts begin early on to institutionalize the program. There are several steps to this process. Perhaps most important is the training of an in-house coach. In some instances, this may be the principal, but other instructional leaders or master teachers also serve this purpose. In some schools and agencies, different personnel become the local expert on different aspects of the program. For example, one person may develop expertise on Haughton's *Phonological Coding* and another may become the Standard Celeration Charting whiz. Yet another person becomes the local expert on assessment.

These people are selected on the basis of their ability to work well with their colleagues. The Morningside coaches and trainers work with these individuals to strengthen their skills as mentors and coaches. The in-house coach may shadow the Morningside coach on several visits and compare notes after the session. On subsequent visits, the in-house coach takes primary responsibility and the Morningside coach serves as his or her coaching coach. Once skills are firm, the in-house coach stays in email and telephone contact with the Morningside coach to check perceptions.

Partner schools are encouraged to identify these in-house coaches early on in the implementation process so they can participate in the Summer School Institute. During the institute, Morningside staff will observe their coaching and provide additional feedback. They also will have the opportunity to observe other expert teachers implement programs and procedure.

A very few teachers, schools, and agencies have agreed to begin remote coaching, later this year, using videotape, I-Cam, and iSight technologies. This is an area that Morningside will be pursuing more diligently in the future, as requests for services come from greater and greater distances.

CHAPTER 11
EMPIRICAL DATA SUPPORTING
TECHNOLOGY TRANSFER OF THE
MORNINGSIDE MODEL OF
GENERATIVE INSTRUCTION

Four features of the Morningside Model constitute the core of the approach. (1) Learner-verified instructional methods, tools, and programs are incorporated for basic academic and learning skill development; (2) A significant amount of school time is allocated to practice using fluency-building and celeration aims; (3) Children learn reasoning, thinking, problem solving, research, and cooperative learning skills; and (4) Children are transitioned into more independent learning environments in which they apply their basic academic, reasoning, research, and cooperative skills to learning social studies, science, and literature according to their interests. Morningside Academy arranges such a learning environment for its children and youth, and they make enormous progress in school.

Parents and leaders in partner schools and agencies are particularly interested in this progress, and they turn almost exclusively to individual student or group performance on standardized tests—macro-level assessment results. In the majority of cases, these are norm-referenced tests, although there is a trend in state-level testing to employ criterion-referenced tests. Morningside teachers are interested in these outcomes as well, because standardized test scores can confirm the changes they are seeing in the classroom. Although the authentic performances that teachers and parents observe socially validate student growth, standardized test scores provide external, independent corroboration of that growth. Remembering Dr. Malmquist's caution in Chapter 4 about the danger of overinterpreting changes in standardized, norm-referenced test scores and the difficulties inherent in age and grade scores, we present the results of standardized measures for the students at Morningside Academy and in our partner schools and agencies.[14]

The remarkable results of Morningside Academy's initial 11-year study of its children's mean standardized test gains in reading, language arts, and mathematics have been reported elsewhere (Johnson & Layng, 1992). Reading averaged 2.5 years growth per school year. By the end of the study, language arts approached an average of four grade levels and mathematics rose to more than three grade levels of improvement per school year. Morningside completed its formal lab school evaluation process in the spring of 1992. Currently it assesses its students in September and June on a variety of in-house, state, and national measures. Children's median achievement test performance remains above two grade levels per year in reading, language arts, and math.

Since 1991 Morningside Teachers' Academy (MTA) has successfully implemented programs in 86 schools and organizations with over 17,000 students in Illinois, Washington, Georgia, Pennsylvania, British Columbia, South Dakota, and Oklahoma. Students in the Chicago Public Schools, the Nechako School District in British Columbia, the Seattle School District, DeKalb County Georgia Public Schools, and elsewhere have profited from our services. MTA has also contracted with several First Nation and American

---

[14] A more thorough assessment of the effects of the Morningside Model of Generative Instruction would include both meta-level assessment data (i.e., CBM data and portfolio products) and micro-level assessment data (i.e., standard celeration chart data), consistent with the assessment model we describe in Chapter 4. Such an evaluation would constitute a monograph or book in and of itself and is beyond the scope of this book. In the interests of those who we believe will be our primary readership, we have analyzed our projects with data they currently find most valuable, macro-level assessment data.

Indian schools in British Columbia, Washington, South Dakota, and Oklahoma, helping them to develop programs in their schools and adult literacy centers. Adult learners in the City Colleges of Chicago and at Motorola Corporation in Phoenix have also made enormous strides in their reading, writing, reasoning, and math skills. A 15% sampling of standardized achievement test results—13 of 86 external partnerships—is presented below.

After Fort Fraser Elementary School, a small rural public school in northern British Columbia, formed a partnership with MTA, students' reading, mathematics, and writing performance improved substantially. Figures 7 and 8 show Fort Fraser student gains in national percentile ranking on the Canadian Test of Basic Skills (CTBS) over a 5-year period. One group of students was tracked from fifth grade through their graduation after seventh grade. Another group was tracked from third grade through their seventh grade graduation. Figure 15 shows changes in reading test scores, and Figure 16 shows changes in mathematics test scores. The 1996 bars in each chart show student performance prior to MTA implementations. 1997–2000 data show student performance after implementing MTA-certified programs, training, and coaching. Both groups made steady gains in both mathematics and reading percentile ranking, achieving scores at the national norms within 2 years. After 4 years, both groups ranked well above average in both reading and math. Since working with MTA, Fort Fraser student performance has risen from a ranking of 13th in a district of 25 schools, to second in math and fifth in reading. Writing performance was systematically measured in 1 year of the project. At the beginning of the year, only 39% of students were at grade level. After 9 months, 80% of students were at grade level.

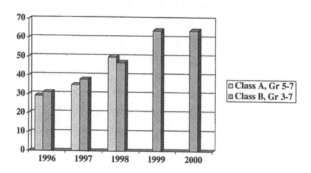

Figure 15. Reading data from a Morningside implementation at Fort Fraser School in British Columbia, Canada.

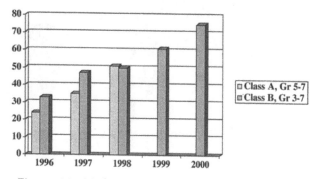

Figure 16. Mathematics data from a Morningside implementation at Fort Fraser School in British Columbia, Canada.

MTA-certified programs have similar effects in the primary grades. Figures 17 and 18 show how the distribution of first grade students' national percentile ranks on reading test scores at Mouse Mountain Primary School in British Columbia shifted in one school year. At the beginning of the school year, over 40% of the students were in the "below average" ($<1^{st}$–29th percentiles) test score range. Over 50% were in the "average" range (30th–70th percentiles). Only 6% were in the "above average" range (71st–99th percentiles). By the end of the school year, the distribution of percentile rankings for the school reversed. There was a 24% decrease in the number of students in the "below average" range, a 10% decrease in the "average" range, and a 35% increase in the "above average" range. This reflects an upward migration of student competencies. Students with below-average scores tended to achieve average scores with MTA reading programs. Students with average scores tended to achieve above-average scores.

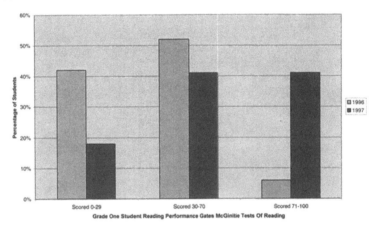

Figure 17. Improvements in national percentile rank in reading following a Morningside implementation among first-grade students at Mouse Mountain primary school in British Columbia, Canada.

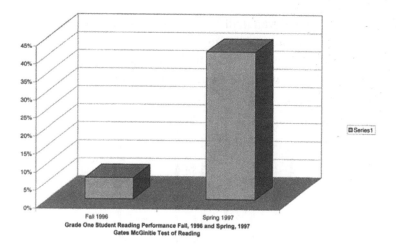

Figure 18. Increases in percentage of students reading "above average" following a Morningside implementation among first-grade students at Mouse Mountain Primary School in British Columbia, Canada.

Morningside Teachers' Academy has similar effects in urban schools. Figures 19, 20, and 21 show Washington Assessment of Student Learning (WASL) results for grade 4 students in three Seattle Public Schools that implemented MTA reading programs. WASL results are reported as the percent of students who met or exceeded ("passed") the state standard. 1999 data in each figure show the results prior to MTA implementation. 2000 and 2001 data show the results after MTA reading programs were implemented.

Each year shows four bars. The first bar indicates the percent of students who passed the reading test. The second bar indicates the percent of students who passed the math test. Since MTA did not implement a math program in these schools, these data serve as a quasi-experimental control.

Thurgood Marshall WASL Reading Achievement
before and during Morningside services
(with TM math, district reading,
and state reading comparisons)

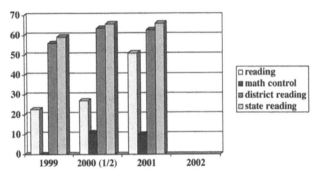

Figure 19. Improvements in reading scores on the
Washington Assessment of Student Learning (WASL)
following a Morningside implementation at Thurgood
Marshall Elementary School in Seattle, WA.

The third bar indicates the percent of students who
passed the reading test across the Seattle School District. The
fourth bar indicates the percent passing the reading test across
Washington State. In each case, (a) substantial gains occurred
after MTA reading was implemented; (b) all three schools were
rapidly approaching average district and state levels; and (c)
math percentages did not increase, providing some confidence
that other changes in the school were not responsible for the
growth in reading achievement. These results are even more
significant when one considers the impoverished economic
levels of students in these schools. Seventy-six percent of
students at Thurgood Marshall qualify for free and reduced
lunch services, 64% at Highland Park qualify, and 81% at
Emerson qualify, compared to 44% in the school district. Only
eight other schools in the district of 115 have 75% or more

students who qualify for free lunch. The average WASL reading gain in those eight schools since the test was instituted in 1998 was 7%. The average WASL reading gain in the three schools that implemented MTA reading programs was 22%.

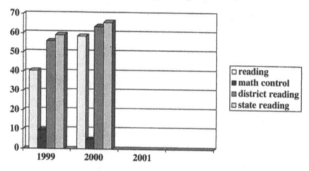

Emerson WASL Reading Achievement
before and during Morningside services
(with Emerson math, district reading,
and state reading comparisons)

Figure 20. Improvements in reading scores on the Washington Assessment of Student Learning (WASL) following a Morningside implementation at Emerson Elementary School in Seattle, WA.

MTA also implemented a summer school skills enhancement program for 176 Seattle Public Schools fifth graders who were at-risk for advancing to middle school. Each student studied two foundations areas (reading, writing, mathematics). In a friendly bet with then-Superintendent John Stanford, MTA was paid $200 above its normal contract fees for each student who gained at least eight months in the 5-week program. Eighty percent (141 students) gained at least 8 months in at least one skill area. Sixty-two percent (110 students) gained at least 8 months in their skill of greatest deficit.

Highland Park WASL Reading Achievement
before and during Morningside services
(with HP math, district reading,
and state reading comparisons)

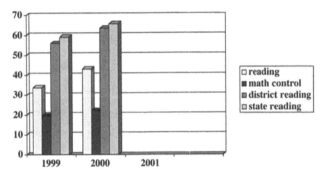

Figure 21. Improvements in reading scores on the Washington Assessment of Student Learning (WASL) following a Morningside implementation at Highland Park Elementary School in Seattle, WA.

Mayor Richard Daley's team invited Morningside Teachers' Academy to participate in the original Chicago Public Schools' Children's First Initiative from 1996–1998. Seventeen schools in the district volunteered to partner with MTA. The Children's First Initiative was perhaps the first district-wide effort to raise student achievement in large inner-city schools by partnering with outside experts. Nineteen external partners joined the Initiative. In an initial pilot project, after 7 months of MTA reading programs, eighth grade students at Carter-Woodson Elementary School in Chicago gained an average of 2.3 grade levels on the Metropolitan Achievement Test 6. Not a single student was at grade level at the start of the program. Within 7 months, 27% of the students were at grade level.

Figures 22, 23, and 24 show student growth in reading on the *Iowa Test of Basic Skills* (ITBS) at 3 other schools in Chicago. At Hearst Elementary School, children were gaining 8 months for every 10 months of reading instruction before MTA. After implementing MTA reading programs, students averaged 12 months gain for 10 months taught. At McKay Elementary School, children were gaining 8 months for every 10 months of reading instruction before MTA. After implementing MTA programs, students averaged 15 months gain for 10 months taught. At Herzl Elementary School, children were gaining 8 months for every 10 months of reading instruction before MTA. After implementing MTA reading programs, students averaged 20 months gain for 10 months taught—a doubling in growth per year.

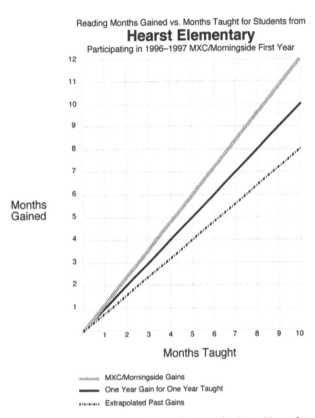

Figure 22. Improvements in reading on the Iowa Test of Basic Skills following a Morningside implementation at Hearst Elementary School in Chicago, IL.

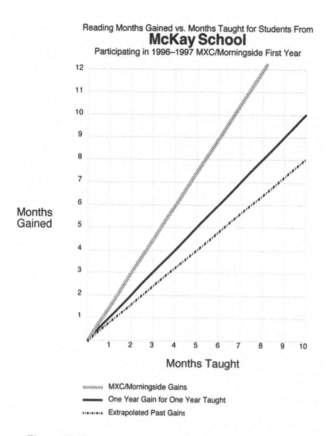

Reading Months Gained vs. Months Taught for Students From
McKay School
Participating in 1996–1997 MXC/Morningside First Year

Figure 23. Improvements in reading on the Iowa Test of Basic Skills following a Morningside implementation at McKay Elementary School in Chicago, IL.

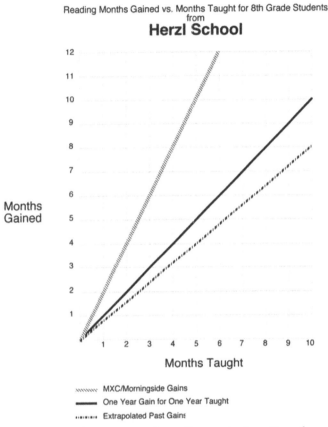

Figure 24. Improvements in reading on the Iowa Test of Basic Skills following a Morningside implementation at Herzl Elementary School in Chicago, IL.

Figures 25 and 26 show the percentage of students that were at or above the 50th percentile in reading comprehension on the *Iowa Test of Basic Skills (ITBS)* in each grade in 2 of the MTA/Chicago partnerships. The first bar for each grade presents the mean percentage of students who were at or above the 50th percentile for a 7-year period (1990–1996) prior to implementing MTA reading programs.

Bontemps Reading Comprehension

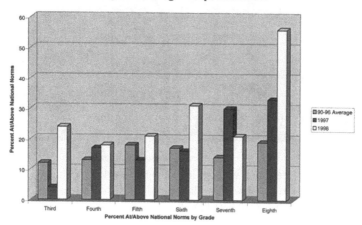

Figure 25. Improvements in reading on the Iowa Test of Basic Skills following a Morningside implementation at Bontemps Elementary School in Chicago, IL.

The second bar for each grade presents the mean percentage of students who were at or above the 50th percentile after 1 year of MTA. The third bar for each grade presents the mean percentage of students who were at or above the 50th percentile after 2 years of MTA. Students at each grade level performed significantly better in 1997, 1998, or both years than they performed in the previous 7 years.

Lathrop School Reading Comprehension

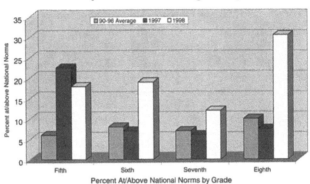

Figure 26. Improvements in reading on the Iowa Test of Basic Skills following a Morningside implementation at Lathrop School in Chicago, IL.

Figure 27 presents summary data in reading comprehension performance averaged across the 17 Chicago Public Schools that partnered with MTA. In general, it can be seen that the students at each grade level performed significantly better in 1997, 1998, or both years than they performed in the previous 7 years.

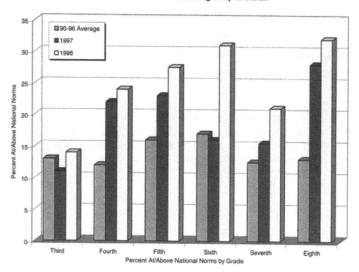

Figure 27. Improvements in reading on the Iowa Test of Basic Skills across all 17 Chicago public schools that implemented the Morningside model.

In a recent partnership with Pine Ridge Indian School in South Dakota, the results after 1 year were very encouraging. Mean percentile scores on the spring 2002 *Stanford Achievement Test 9 (SAT-9)* indicate that all grades made improvements in reading achievement. Student performance in each grade was compared with their performance in the previous grade, approximating a within-group analysis. Figure 28 shows three grades that showed substantial gains in national percentile ranks. First graders made almost 2 years' growth, increasing from the 27th percentile in kindergarten to the 41st percentile in first grade, a 14-percentile point increase. Third graders made more than 1 year's growth, increasing from the 26th percentile in second grade to the 34th percentile in third grade, an 8 percentile point increase. Sixth graders also made more than 1 year's growth, increasing from the 22nd percentile in fifth grade to the 31st percentile in sixth grade, a 9 percentile point increase. It is very unusual for students performing in the first quartile to make such large gains. These data reverse the long-term trend at Pine Ridge of declining achievement in reading as one advances from grade to grade.

Pine Ridge Indian School
Average national percentile rank in reading achievement, SAT-9.
Students' current performance with Morningside Reading for 4
months compared with their performance in the previous grade
before Morningside.

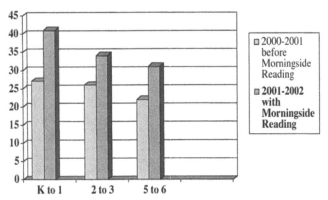

Figure 28. Improvements in the 2002 Stanford Achievement Test following a Morningside implementation at Pine Ridge Indian School in South Dakota.

We currently have partnerships with two other Bureau of Indian Affairs (BIA) schools. Over 400 elementary, middle, and high school students at Riverside Indian School in Anadarko, Oklahoma are participating in our reading programs. Students enrolled in a smaller school in South Dakota's capitol, Pierre Learning Center, are also participating in our reading program. We expect similar reading achievement gains from these students this spring. At least four other BIA schools have expressed serious interest in a partnership with Morningside Teachers' Academy.

Results are even more striking for adult learners (see Figure 29). For example, in our first adult literacy program at the Morningside Academy lab school, KR gained 42 months or 4 years and 2 months in math on the Metropolitan Achievement Test after just two months of instruction, moving from a 6.9 grade level to an 11.1 grade level. WB gained 27 months or 2 years and 7 months in math after just a month and a half of instruction, moving from an 8.1 grade level to a 10.8 grade level. DM gained 84 months or 8 years and 4 months in reading after just a month of reading instruction, moving from a 3.6 grade level to a post high school grade level. JK gained 72 months or 7 years and 2 months in written language after just 3 months of instruction, moving from an 5.8 grade level to a post high school grade level. These results have been replicated in numerous projects. Wherever Morningside has implemented an adult literacy program, be it in a community college such as Malcolm X College in Chicago, a state university such as Jacksonville State University in Alabama, or a manufacturing company such as Motorola Corporation in Phoenix, learners have gained approximately two grades per month of instruction (Johnson & Layng, 1992, 1994).

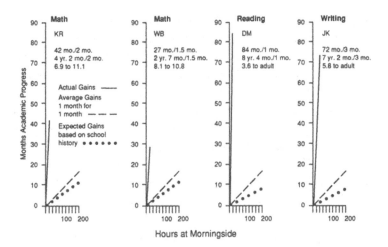

Figure 29. Progress of four adult learners on the Metropolitan Achievement Test at Morningside Academy in Seattle, WA.

CHAPTER 12
FROM THE FIELD TO THE LABORATORY

As we have noted in the preface to this book, Morningside Academy is a laboratory school in which scientifically validated curricular, management, and instructional elements are combined and recombined to produce anticipated student gains on specified outcomes. In setting after setting with children and adolescents who have struggled academically, our instructional protocols are effective. Our combination of standard celeration charting with a changing criterion design provides evidence that students are learning. Further, their learning is greatly accelerated over that which they were achieving before they entered our laboratory school or one of our partner schools or agencies.

As a field based laboratory school, we rarely do bench science; that is, we rarely test individual elements of our curricular and instructional protocols to determine their relative contributions toward our overall success. We don't systematically vary procedures in a rigorous experimental design. To put some perspective on this, we refer to Dr. Jim Johnston's (1996) perspective. He asserts that applied research is much closer in nature to basic research than it is to service settings such as Morningside whose priority is to deliver an effective service to solve real-world problems. Service settings should not be expected to create the contrived circumstances necessary for applied research. These may include modification of the setting and the use of non-indigenous subjects to come into line with more basic research findings and to rule out alternative explanations. Such changes compromise the power of service settings to solve problems. Nor should "features of an applied context take precedence over methodological needs" when conducting applied research (p. 42). The development of a truly applied research literature that seamlessly dovetails with basic research lies at the heart of the development of technology and technology transfer. In behavior analysis as a discipline we agree with Dr. Johnston that there is an over-reliance on "applied research" in real-world settings that has compromised the development of technology and technology transfer, as well as compromised the solution of real-world problems in those service settings that attempt to do both.

In other words, as in the application of engineering and medical technologies, practice is generally not an occasion for discovering, understanding, or explaining in a scientific sense. Although individual practitioners may gain from experience in these ways, such knowledge is quite different than that obtained by researchers and cannot substitute for applied research. It is a mistake to view the circumstances of service delivery as accommodating the applied research agenda on a systematic basis (p. 44).

As an extension of Dr. Johnston's perspective, we propose three levels of scientifically driven organizations. Morningside Academy and its partner schools illustrate level 3, service delivery organizations. In level 3 organizations, macro-level outcome research is necessary to validate applications. Level 3 organizations also collect meta and micro level data, which provides continuous and formative feedback about their successes and challenges, but it is not as systematic as is required by applied research. Level 2 organizations are true applied research facilities that make the necessary compromises to align with basic research. Their primary purpose is not to deliver service to solve practical problems, although they may often do so. They would exist primarily to do research to understand "the mechanism of a procedure's action, rather than its apparent effectiveness" (Johnston, 1996, p. 40). This is what qualifies a procedure or program as a technology and readies it for technology transfer. Level 1 organizations are devoted to basic research, and would currently be found mostly in university departments. In the future behavior technology may imitate medical technology in which case research organizations may spawn outside of university settings.

As we apply scientific research to real-world concerns, we feel we are recapturing the original intent of laboratory schools: to test applied research findings through application in a complex environment, on the one hand, and to pose interesting questions to level 2 and 1 organizations, on the other hand. This interplay between field-based settings and the research laboratory ensures that basic research is helping to achieve solutions to authentic problems and that application is grounded in scientific study. As a level 3 organization Morningside Academy is well-prepared to generate interesting and important research questions for level 2 and 1 organizations to investigate.

Thus, we end this book with a set of questions for which basic and applied research is needed to inform our practice. We've organized the questions around six themes:

Assessment

As we describe in Chapter 4, Morningside adopts three levels of assessment: macro, meta, and micro. The macro level assessment is most like what measurement experts call summative assessment, assessment that judges growth at the end of a course of study. It occurs once yearly and typically is norm-referenced. Measures are typically highly standardized and widely accepted in the field of assessment and evaluation. The meta level assesses growth periodically throughout the year and uses instruments that are correlated with the curriculum and that typically provide social validation of student growth. Morningside uses an adaptation of the

Curriculum-Based Measurement (CBM) strategies developed by Deno (1985), Shinn (1989), and others for this purpose. Unlike test scores, which require a great deal of technical expertise to be fully understood and to avoid misinterpretation, these meta-level assessments show the learner engaged in authentic tasks that communicate to the casual observer that improvements are occurring. Typically, these measures are both formative and summative. They are formative in the sense that they provide diagnostic information for the teacher; they are summative in the sense that they sum up performance at predesignated periods throughout the year. The third type of assessment, the micro level, measures performance daily on a series of component skills that are thought to combine in ways that improve student performance on the authentic tasks that make up the meta-level assessment.

At Morningside, when performance at each more microscopic level doesn't appear to be validated by performance on macro level assessment, teachers and designers refine task analyses, make program changes, or adopt a macro-level test that corresponds more directly to the curriculum. However, all of this has been done without benefit of an empirical analysis of the three levels of assessment and the degree to which each level predicts the next. This is a rich area for research and would be enormously helpful to practitioners.

Inductive and Deductive Educational Practice

In the case of reading instruction, our reviewer Phil Chase (2004) precisely described the research question here. He told us:

> I think it might be logical to say that (sight word reading instruction) is less efficient (than phonetic components reading instruction) as a generative process,

but by learning many sight words children might learn to induce the decoding rules that experts have already induced. When the problem is looked at from this perspective, decoding becomes a rule governed, expository, deductive method for teaching aspects of reading and sight reading becomes a contingency governed, discovery, inductive method of teaching reading, and the jury is still out on which teaches more or better generativity. Most studies of these variables suggest that the former is more efficient, but the latter is more likely to produce the response variation that is critical under new (i.e., generative) situations.

Fluency

Definition

Fluency is defined in many different ways. Cognitive psychologists focus upon automaticity and amount of "attention" required to perform a task or to solve a problem. Educational psychologists have restricted the fluency domain to reading performance. Behavior analysts have specified multiple learning outcomes necessary to call any performance truly fluent (RESAA: retention, endurance, stability, application and adduction). Research comparing data produced by each of these research groups would yield ever more interesting questions about highly skilled performance.

Performance Rate as an Indicator of Retention, Endurance, Stability, Application, and Adduction (RESAA)

Morningside uses an approach to practice, Precision Teaching, that assumes that rate of responding is itself a critical predictor of RESAA. That is, it assumes that rate of responding adds power over accuracy of responding, and that number of trials alone does not predict fluency. A number of behavior analysts and educational researchers have challenged

211

this assertion, citing insufficient evidence of its effectiveness. Precision Teachers and other rate-building enthusiasts counter that while there is no evidence, rate building is preferable because it is considerably more efficient than a slow trial-by-trial practice. However, some opponents say the approach is unnecessarily stress-producing and that the anxiety that results isn't worth the time savings.

About a dozen studies have been conducted to test student performance RESAA as a function of the frequency with which they could perform the skill at an earlier point in time, thus determining to what extent frequency predicts retention, endurance, stability and application (Binder, 1996). The problem with all but one of these studies is that appropriate control conditions for comparison have not been established. Many times the amount of practice is typically larger in the fluency condition, so one could say that amount of practice alone can produce retention, endurance, stability, and application. Many times the amount of practice between fluency and control groups is equal but the average frequency of the control group's performance equals the fluency group, eliminating a basis of comparison. Sometimes the fluency aim selected is too low, in our estimation, to produce RESAA.

Research Design

Below we describe seven control conditions that should be included in research on fluency.

- Any subjects whose performance is being compared to subjects who receive frequency building must be given the same number of total practice opportunities, or at least the same amount of practice time. Yoked control procedures show promise.

- Before testing for RESAA both experimental and control subjects must be tested with free-operant methods to determine that all of the experimental subjects perform at or above the frequency aim, and all of the control subjects perform significantly below the frequency aim.

- Frequency-building procedures should begin with performances that are already established; that is, firm at frequencies between 10 and 20 correct per minute, with no errors.

- No feedback of any kind should be given between performances during the timing period.

- Stimuli should be presented in an array that permits the subject to move from one task to another without experimenter intervention; i.e., no trials procedures.

- When using matching-to-sample arrangements, omit public demonstration of an observing response to the sample, as it will put a ceiling on the frequency that may be required to demonstrate RESAA.

- Before one compares fluent and non-fluent performance with novel or arbitrary stimuli, one must do a pre-study, determining the frequency aim necessary for performance to meet RESAA criteria. (See Fabrizio & Moors, 2003 for a demonstration.) Frequency aims for the fluency and non-fluency subjects can then be set accordingly.

Frequency Plus

Beginning with the assumption that behavioral fluency as defined by retention, endurance, stability, application, and adduction is an important outcome of education, it would be extraordinarily helpful to determine what characteristics of practice performance predict fluency.

Setting Aims

Most of us have set aims for instructional objectives or pinpoints, creating a never-ending task for the near-infinite number of objectives in the academic world. Perhaps the daunting nature of such a time and effort-consuming approach has discouraged such precise and systematic effort. After all we have students to teach, interventions to try, and so on. However, recently Fabrizio and Moors (2003) set aims for learning channels, not instructional objectives, and empirically tested their effects with autistic students. The much more finite set of learning channels makes the empirical effort of aim setting doable. However, the generalizability of the method of setting performance aims by learning channels may be subject to other features of a pinpoint. As one of us said in a published review of their article (Johnson, 2003):

> Fabrizio and Moors' (2003) learning channels and tasks show a tight correspondence between the activity in the "input" and the activity in the "output." For examples, the teacher's activity in "hear/say sounds" is identical to the student's activity. The teacher presents an animal picture in "see/say animals by name" and the student says its name. The teacher demonstrates a gross motor skill in "see/do gross motor imitation" and the student imitates it.
>
> The more complex range of objectives typical of general education objectives may not align so neatly by learning channel. In general education we sometimes have the type of objectives represented in the Fabrizio/Moors curriculum; we call them tool skills. For example, in our writing curriculum at Morningside Academy we include the pinpoint, "see/write text." This one is similar to the pinpoints in the Fabrizio/Moors curriculum. We also have other "see/write" objectives in which the "input" and the "output" do not line up so tightly. For examples, in "see/write combined sentences" what occurs in the "see" is a set of short choppy

sentences. What occurs in the "write" is a longer complex sentence made from the short choppy sentences. This pinpoint has a much lower frequency aim than the tool skill aim. Another "see/write" in our curriculum is "see/write persuasive paragraphs." This "see/write" has a substantially different frequency aim from "see/write combined sentences." My observation is not a criticism of the Fabrizio/Moors effort, rather it is a refinement of their learning channels approach to defining aims. Perhaps with a wider range of objectives typical of general education and business and industry objectives and pinpoints we will discover three or four levels of learning channel aims that can neatly attach to three or four levels of objectives. (p. 68)

Effect of Goal Setting on Celeration

Proponents of Precision Teaching set performance aims based on a suggested relation between a particular rate of responding and RESAA. However, some proponents also have suggested that communicating a daily performance aim to the learner results in faster progress toward the eventual performance aim. In current practice many teachers draw an anticipated celeration line on the daily Standard Celeration Chart to establish expected progress from baseline performance to an eventual performance aim. Daily goals are then derived from these celeration lines. For many years, celeration lines reflected an expectation that performance would grow 1.25 times per week. That is, if performance begins at 100 movements per minute, after one week of practice, one could reasonably expect performance at 125 movements per minute. As evidence mounted that student growth was routinely exceeding the projected celeration line, Lindsley and others began to experiment with steeper celeration lines, and expected growth to double or triple across a week of practice on well-defined curriculum slices. Morningside Academy set a celeration aim of x2 for most of its pinpoints in the early

1980s, and redesigned instructional programs and protocols as necessary to produce these results.

More recently, some teachers have suggested that while celeration lines and daily goals derived from them may stimulate faster growth, they may also dampen growth. This presents an interesting question for controlled empirical research: In what ways does goal-setting in Precision Teaching affect celeration?

David Letterman Revisited

Our Top Ten fluency research questions line up like this:

10—What is the relation between different frequency aims and performance endurance?

9—What is the relation between frequency aims and remembering? Are there differences for different types of remembering (after Donahoe & Palmer, 1994)?

8—What is the relation between frequency aims and performance stability?

7—What is the relation between performance stability and endurance? Are they the same or different phenomena?

6—What is the relation between the frequency aims necessary for fluency, and *celeration aims*? Is it true that performances with steeper celeration slopes on Standard Celeration Charts will be fluent at lower frequency aims than performances that have more gradual celeration slopes? More generally, is it true that the faster one reaches the fluency aim, the lower the frequency aim one needs to reach?

5—What is the relation between error frequencies during performance instruction and the frequency aim needed for fluency? Is it true that the fewer the errors produced during instruction, the lower one can set the frequency aim to produce fluency?

4—What is the relation between component and composite performance frequencies? Are they arithmetically, geometrically, or exponentially related? Do the relations change across the spectrum of frequencies?

3—What are effective peer frequency-building procedures to use in the classroom or work setting?

2—What are the most powerful arrangements of practice materials, specifically spaced and cumulative practice procedures? Is it true that one can set lower frequency aims with better spaced and cumulative practice materials?

1—What is the relation between frequency aims and contingency adduction? Do higher frequency performances squeeze out competing contingencies? Is it true that frequency building produces repertoires that require less instruction as one proceeds up a curriculum ladder or through a behavior sequence of increasing complexity? Under what conditions do frequency building and fluency procedures facilitate or inhibit creativity, problem–solving, and expert performance? Will setting empirically derived fluency aims affect the amount or kind of deliberate practice (after Eriksson, Krampe, & Tesch-Romer, 1993) required to become an expert?

Thinking Aloud Problem Solving (TAPS)

Whimbey and others have demonstrated that they can improve problem-solving and reasoning abilities of college students through the use of a systematic thinking aloud problem solving (TAPS) approach. However, much of the data uses pre- to post-test gains, and the model has not been subjected to a rigorous experimental test. At Morningside, students' standardized test scores have improved since TAPS was introduced, but its introduction has coincided with other curricular and instructional program changes. At this time, then, it's not clear why or how TAPS works, if exposure to problem solving and reasoning activities alone would have a similar impact on performance, or which of its several components contribute to its overall effectiveness. Further, its function as a process repertoire that recruits and blends component skills as needed to engage in a novel performance remains to be empirically tested.

TAPS is an area ripe for research, particularly during a time when there is a call in educational and training circles for efficient and elegant programs that will improve problem solving and reasoning.

Data Collection

At Morningside, teachers collect performance data on students and use the data to modify the curriculum and instructional practices. These data-collection and analysis protocols have been relatively easy to institute for tool skill instruction in which one and only one right answer is correct. However, as we have begun to develop protocols for teaching composite and complex skills that provide the learner more latitude in the "answer"—for example, a comprehension skill such as inference—we have been challenged to develop data collection approaches that are elegant and that inspire teachers to make qualitative judgments as well as quantitative ones. Currently, we are attempting to develop a tracking system for the delayed prompting technique, in which teachers judge not only the accuracy of the student's response, but also the level and type of their own prompts.

An example might help to clarify the dilemma. Teachers introduce approximately 20 comprehension skills to students one at a time by providing definitions of the skill and modeling its use in the context of group story reading. Teachers then provide opportunities over many days following introduction for each student to demonstrate the skill. In the delayed prompting technique, the teacher withholds prompts until a period of time has passed following an instruction at which time he or she introduces a light prompt, followed by heavier and heavier prompts as the student's performance requires. The formal properties of the answer will vary considerably and still meet the requirements of the task. In fact, to be judged a correct response, an answer should not correspond point to point to models provided by the teacher or other students. When students have successfully responded without prompts to several opportunities to demonstrate a particular comprehension skill, the teacher shifts to a new one for that student. However, simultaneously, other students in the class may still be learning how to respond to the first comprehension skill or may continue to be dependent on prompts. The teacher may have many students in the group, sometimes up to 20 or more, and must track each student's performance within and across the skills and across many days and many stories.

We believe it is important to develop elegant data collection systems for these complicated circumstances. We have toyed with the idea of a computer-based approach, but have not yet discovered something that is easy for teachers to use and that is portable. We also are interested in ensuring that the data collection protocol doesn't divert the teacher's attention away from making qualitative judgments of students' answers. For example, if a student gives a technically correct response, but is hesitant, we want the teacher to continue to pursue the skill with the student until his response is firm. We also know that teachers won't take data if the data-collection system is cumbersome. To solve these important problems, we recommend research that both develops a data collection system that is teacher-friendly and that socially validates teachers' assessments.

The Daily Report Card

At Morningside Academy laboratory school, instructional services are couched in a token economy system in the form of a daily report card. Students earn points and privileges for academic, organizational, learning skills and citizenship aims. These points are often backed up by more concrete rewards on some daily or weekly cycle. Behavioral researchers could help us discover the relative effects of superimposing a token economy point system upon student achievement and satisfaction.

Summary

At Morningside, we will continue to modify curriculum, instructional practices, and assessment protocols to achieve promised educational outcomes. However, we will continue to be a level 3 scientifically driven organization, dependent on levels 1 and 2 organizations to help us understand which of our complex package of strategies contribute to our success and how much each contributes. Because our goal is to help students catch up and move ahead, we are eager to streamline daily practice to achieve greater efficiency. We have been open to practices that have arisen from a variety of philosophic orientations and will continue to be, so long as evidence suggests their effectiveness and they protect the dignity of our students. If in reading this account of interesting research questions, you wish to engage us in conversation about them, we would be glad to partner with you to design research protocols to answer them.

AFTERWORD

Morningside has more than 20 years of commitment to the ideals of educational accountability and empirically verified approaches to instruction, one that places the responsibility for student success squarely on the shoulders of educators. Schools should not act as mere sorting machines for determining degrees of natural, genetic, or preexisting talent. A growing emphasis in recent years on student test scores has redirected teachers' energies away from their primary charge: to provide programs that meet the educational and life needs of all children. Performance on tests may provide some evidence that the schools are meeting this need, but they are not the only evidence schools should seek. Beyond increasing their test scores, schools must act so that all children are literate and can function as effective citizens in a democracy.

We've inherited children who have been left behind, and we've helped them catch up and move ahead. We've believed that if the child wasn't learning, we weren't teaching. We've included learners in the teaching process, as coaches with each other. We've reformed our practices until the evidence reveals that our practices work for learners. And we've shared the effective practices with others whose children were left behind. We've stood behind our practices, offering families money-back learning guarantees. In the end we believe we've helped define what it means to leave no child behind.

REFERENCES

Alessi, G. (1987). Generative strategies and teaching for generalization. *The Analysis of Verbal Behavior*, 5, 15–27.

Anderson, J. R., Reder, L. M., & Simon, H. A. (1996). Situated learning and education. *Educational Researcher*, 25, 5–11.

Andronis, P. T., Layng, T. V. J., & Goldiamond, I. (1997). Contingency adduction of "symbolic aggression" by pigeons. *The Analysis of Verbal Behavior*, 14, 5–17.

Archer, A. (2002). An instructional approach to teaching written composition. An unpublished developmental draft.

Barrett, B. H. (2003). *The Technology of Teaching revisited: A reader's companion to B. F. Skinner's book.* Cambridge, MA: Cambridge Center for Behavioral Studies.

Bennett , B. (1987). The effectiveness of staff development training practices: A meta-analysis. Doctoral dissertation, University of Oregon.

Berk, L. E. (1994, November). Why children talk to themselves. *Scientific American, 271(5)*, 78–83.

Beyer, B. K. (1997). *Improving student thinking.* Needham, MA: Allyn & Bacon.

Binder, C V. (1988). Precision teaching: Measuring and attaining academic excellence. *Youth Policy, 10*, 12–15.

Binder, C. V. (1993, October). Behavioral fluency: A new paradigm. *Education Technology, 8–14.*

Binder, C. V. (1996). Behavioral fluency: Evolution of a new paradigm. *The Behavior Analyst, 19, 163–197.*

Bloom, B. S. (1950). Problem-solving processes of college students: An exploratory investigation. Chicago, IL: Supplemental Educational Monographs. The School

Review and the Elementary School Journal, 75,
University of Chicago Press.
Bringmann, W., Luck, H., Miller, R., & Early, C. (Eds.).
(1997). *A pictorial history of psychology.* Chicago:
Quintessence.
Camilli, T. (1992). *A case of red herrings: Solving mysteries through
critical questioning.* Pacific Grove, CA: Critical Thinking
Books & Software.
Carnine, D., Silbert, J., & Kameenui, E. J., (1990), *Direct
instruction reading.* Columbus, OH: Merrill.
Catania, A. C. (1975). The myth of self-reinforcement.
Behaviorism, 3, 192–199.
Chase, P. (2004). Personal communication.
Daiker, D. A., Kerek, A. & Morenberg, M. (1979). *The writer's
option: College sentence combining.* New York: Harper &
Row.
Deno, S. L. (1985). Curriculum-based measurement: The
emerging alternative. *Exceptional Children, 52,* 219–
232.
Deno, S. L. (1986). Formative evaluation of individual student
programs: A new role for school psychologists. *School
Psychology Review, 15,* 358–374.
Deno, S. L. (1989). Curriculum-based measurement and
special education services: A fundamental and direct
relationship. In M. R. Shinn (Ed.), *Curriculum-based
measurement: Assessing special children* (pp. 1–17). New
York: Guilford Press.
Deno, S. (1992). The nature and development of curriculum-
based measurement. *Preventing School Failure, 36(2),* 5–
10.
Dewey, J. (1900). *The school and society.* Chicago: University of
Chicago Press.
Dewey, J. (1902). *The child and the curriculum.* Chicago:

University of Chicago Press.

Dewey, J. (1916). *Democracy and education: An introduction to the philosophy of education.* New York: The Free Press.

Dewey, J. (1933). *How we think.* In J. Dewey (1986) *The Later Works of John Dewey, 1925–1953,* Vol. 8, Carbondale: Southern Illinois University Press.

Dewey, J. (1938). *Experience and education.* New York: Collier Books, Macmillan Publishing Company.

Dewey, J. (1986). *John Dewey: The later works, 1925–1953.* Carbondale, IL: Southern Illinois University Press.

Diamond, J. (1997). *Guns, germs, and steel: The fates of human societies.* New York: W. W. Norton.

Ellson, D. G. (1969). *Harper-Row tutorial: Tutor's guide experimental edition.* Bloomington, IN: Department of Psychology, Indiana University.

Engelmann, S., & Carnine, D. W. (1982). *Theory of instruction: Principles and applications.* New York: Irvinston.

Epstein, R. (1991). Skinner, creativity, and the problem of spontaneous behavior. *Psychological Science, 2,* 362–370.

Epstein, R., Kirshnit, R., Lanza, R., & Rubin, R. (1984). "Insight" in the pigeon: Antecedents and determinants of an intelligent performance. *Nature, 308,* 61–62.

Ericsson, K. A., Krampe, R Th., & Tesch-Romer, C. (1993). The role of deliberate practice in the acquisition of expert performance. *Psychological Review, 100* (3), 363–406.

Evans, J. L., Homme, L. E., & Glaser, R. (1962). The RULEG system for the construction of programmed verbal learning sequences. *Journal of Educational Research, 55,* 513–518.

Evans (1968). *B. F. Skinner: The man and his ideas.* New York: E. P. Dutton.

Fabrizio, M. A., & Moors, A. L. (2003). Evaluating mastery:

Measuring instructional outcomes for children with
autism. *European Journal of Behavior Analysis*, *3* (1 & 2),
23–36.

Ferster, C. (1965). Verbal behavior as magic. Paper presented
at the 50th Anniversary Conference of the Graduate
School of Education, the University of Pennsylvania. In
Ferster, C. B., Culbertson, S. and Boren, M. C. P.,
Behavior principles (2nd Ed.). (pp. 563–568). Engelwood
Cliffs, NJ: Prentice-Hall, 1975.

Ferster, C. (1967). Arbitrary and natural reinforcement.
Psychological Record, 17, 341–347.

Ferster, C., (1972). Clinical reinforcement. *Seminars in
Psychiatry, 4*, 101–111.

Ferster, C., B., & Culbertson, S. (1974). A psychology learning
center. *Psychological Record, 24*, 33–46.

Finn, C. E., & Ravitch, D. (1996). *Education reform: 1995–96*.
A Report from the Educational Excellence Network to
its Education Policy Committee and the American
People.

Flesch, R. (1951). *The art of clear thinking*. New York: Harper
and Row.

Fox, L. (1962). Effecting the use of efficient study habits.
Journal of Mathetics, 1, 75–86.

Fuchs, L. S., Hamlett, C. L., & Fuchs, D. (1997). *Monitoring
basic skills progress*. (2nd ed.). Austin: Pro-Ed.

Gagne, R. (1965). *The conditions of learning*. New York: Holt,
Rinehart, and Winston.

Gagne, R. (1970). *The conditions of learning* (2nd ed.). New
York: Holt, Rinehart, and Winston.

Gagne, R. (1977). *The conditions of learning* (3rd ed.). New York:
Holt, Rinehart, and Winston.

Gagne, R. (1985). *The conditions of learning* (4th ed.). New York:
Holt, Rinehart, and Winston.

Gilbert, T (1962a). Mathetics: The technology of education. *Journal of Mathetics, 1* (1), 7–74.

Gilbert, T. (1962b). Mathetics II: The design of teaching exercises. *Journal of Mathetics, 1* (1), 7–56.

Goldiamond, I. (1976). Self-reinforcement. *Journal of Applied Behavior Analysis, 9,* 509–514.

Graff, S. & Lindsley, O. R. (2002). Standard celeration charting, 2002. Poland, OH: Graf Implements.

Graf, S. (2000). *How to develop, produce, and use SAFMEDS in education and training, V 4.3.* Youngstown, Ohio: Zero Brothers Software.

Haughton, E. (1972). Aims: Growing and sharing. In J. B. Jordan and L. S. Robbins (Eds.). *Let's Try Doing Something Else Kind of Thing.* (pp. 20–39). Arlington, VA: Council for Exceptional Children.

Haughton, E. (1980). Practicing practices: Learning by activity. *Journal of Precision Teaching, 1,* 3–20.

Haughton, E. (1999). *Phonemic awareness: Phonological coding: Phonemic awareness* (2nd ed.). Napa, CA: Haughton Learning Center.

Haughton, E. (2003). *Rapid automatic naming (RAN).* Napa, CA: Haughton Learning Center.

Heiman, M., & Slominko, J. (1985). *Critical thinking skills.* Washington, DC: National Education Association Publication.

Heiman, M., & Slomianko, J. (1988). *Methods of inquiry and technology of change.* Cambridge, MA: Learning to Learn, Inc.

Howell, K. W., Fox, S. L., & Moorehead, M. K. (1993). *Curriculum-based evaluation: Teaching and decision making* (2nd ed). Pacific Grove, CA: Brooks/Cole.

Johnson, K. (2001, May). Ten dimensions of reading. Association for Behavior Analysis, Toronto, Canada.

THE MORNINGSIDE MODEL

Workshop: Teaching Reading with the Morningside
Model of Generative Instruction.

Johnson, K. (2004). *The daily report card*. Seattle: Morningside
Press.

Johnson, K. (2003). Contributions of precision teaching.
European Journal of Behavior Analysis, 4, 66–70.

Johnson, K. R., & Layng, T. V. J. (1992). Breaking the
structuralist barrier: Literacy and numeracy with
fluency. *American Psychologist, 47*, 1475–1490.

Johnson, K. R., & Layng, T. V. J. (1994). The Morningside
Model of Generative Instruction. In R. Gardner, D.
Sainato, J. Cooper, T. Heron, W. Heward, J.
Eshleman, and T. Grossi (Eds.), *Behavior analysis in
education: Focus on measurably superior instruction*. (pp.
173-197). Belmont CA: Brooks-Cole.

Johnson, K. R., & Layng, T. V. J. (1996). On terms and
procedures: Fluency. *The Behavior Analyst, 19*, 281–
288.

Johnson, K., & Street, E. M. (2004). The Morningside Model
of Generative Instruction: An integration of research-
based practices. In D. J. Moran & R. Malott (Eds.).
Empirically supported educational methods. St. Louis, MO:
Elsevier Science/Academic Press.

Johnston, J. M. (1996). Distinguishing between applied
research and practice. *The Behavior Analyst, 19* (1), 35–
47.

Joyce, B., & Showers, B. (1995). *Student achievement through staff
development: Fundamentals of staff development*. White
Plains, NY: Longman Publishers.

Keller, F. S. (1968). "Goodbye, teacher. . ." *Journal of Applied
Behavior Analysis, 1*, 79–89.

Keller, F. S., & Sherman, J. G. (1974). *The Keller plan handbook*.
Menlo Park: W. A. Benjamin.

Knutson, N., & Shinn, M. R. (1991). Curriculum-based

measurement: Conceptual underpinnings and integration into problem-solving assessment. *Journal of School Psychology, 29,* 371–393.

Kozloff, M.A., Lanunziata, L., Cowardin, J., & Bessellieu, F. (2001). Direct instruction: Its contributions to high school achievement. *The High School Journal, 84,* 54–71.

Kuhn, M. R., & Stahl, S. A. (2003). Fluency: A review of developmental and remedial practices. *Journal of Educational Psychology, 95,* 3–21.

Layng, T. V. J., Twyman, J. S., & Stikeleather, G. (2004). Engineering discovery learning: The contingency adduction of some precursors of textual responding in a beginning reading program. *The Analysis of Verbal Behavior, 20,* 99–109.

Layng, T. V. J., Stikeleather, G., & Twyman, J. S. (2004). Scientific formative evaluation: The role of individual learners in generating and predicting successful educational outcomes. In: Subotnik, R., & Walberg, H. (Eds.) *The Scientific Basis of Educational Productivity.* Washington, D.C.: American Psychological Association.

LeStorti, A. (2000). Developing thinking in the gifted. Pennsylvania Association for the Gifted. http://www.penngifted.org/bulletins/b3.html. Retrieved, February, 2004.

Linden, M., & Whimbey, A. (1990). *Why Johnny can't write.* Hillsdale, New Jersey: Lawrence Erlbaum Associates.

Lindsley, O. R. (1971). Precision teaching in perspective: An interview with Ogden R. Lindsley. *Teaching Exceptional Children, 3(3),* 114–119.

Lindsley, O. R. (1972). From Skinner to precision teaching: The child knows best. In J. B. Jordan and L. S. Robbins (Eds.). *Let's try doing something else kind of thing* (pp. 1–11). Arlington, VA: Council for Exceptional Children.

Lindsley, O. R. (1990). Precision teaching: By teachers for children. *Teaching Exceptional Children*, 22 (3), 10-15.

Lovitt, T. C., & Horton, S. V. (1991). Adapting textbooks for mildly handicapped adolescents. In G. Stoner, M. R. Shinn, & H. M. Walker (Eds.), *Interventions for achievement and behavior problems* (pp 439–472). Silver Springs, MD: National Association for School Psychologists.

Markle, S. M. (1967). Empirical testing of programs. In P.C. Lange (Ed.). *Programmed instruction: Sixty-sixth yearbook of the national society for the study of education: 2* (pp. 104–138). Chicago: University of Chicago Press.

Markle, S. M. (1969) *Good frames and bad: A grammar of frame writing* (2nd ed.). New York: Wiley.

Markle, S. M. (1990). *Designs for instructional designers.* Champaign, IL: Stipes.

Markle, S. M., & Croege, S. (1980, February). Solving the problem of problem solving domains. *NSPI Journal,* 30–33.

Markle, S. M., & Tiemann, P. W. (1967). Programming is a process. (Film.) Chicago: University of Illinois.

Marston, D. (1989). Curriculum-based measurement: What is it and why do it? In M. R. Shinn (Ed.), *Curriculum-based measurement: Assessing special children* (pp. 18–78). New York: Guilford Press.

Nelson, R. O., & Hayes, S. C., (1986). The nature of behavioral assessment. In R.O. Nelson & S.C. Hayes (Eds.), *Conceptual foundations of behavioral assessment* (pp. 3–41). New York: Guilford Press.

O'Hare, F. (1973). *Sentence combining: Improving student writing without formal grammar instruction.* Urbana, IL: National Council of Teachers of English.

Osman, M., & Hannafin, M. J. Effects of advance questioning and prior knowledge on science learning. *Journal of Educational Research, 88,* 5–13.

Packer, M. J., & Goicoechea, J. (2000). Sociocultural and constructivist theories of learning: Ontology, not just epistemology. *Educational Psychologist, 35,* 227–241.

Palmer, D. A. (1991). Behavioral interpretation of memory. In P. Chase and L. Hayes, (Eds.). *Dialogues on verbal behavior.* Reno, NV: Context Press.

Pennypacker, H. S., Gutierrez, A., & Lindsley, O. R. (2003). *Handbook of the Standard Celeration Chart, Deluxe Edition.* Available at http://www.behavior.org.

Phillips, D. C. (1995). The good, the bad, and the ugly: The many faces of constructivism. *Educational Researcher, 24,* 5–12.

Phillips, D. C. (1997). How, why, what, when, and where: Perspectives on constructivism and education. *Issues in Education: Contributions from Educational Psychology, 3,* 151–194.

Piaget, J. (1972). *Insights and illusions of philosophy.* New York: Routledge and Kegan Paul.

Pressley, M, & Harris, K. R. (1997). Constructivism and instruction. *Issues in Education, 3, 245–255.*

Richardson, V. (1997). Constructivist teaching and teacher education: Theory and practice. In V. Richardson (Ed.) *Constructivist teacher education: Building new understandings.* Washington, DC: The Falmer Press.

Robbins, J. K., Layng, T. V. J., & Jackson, P. J. (1995). *Fluent thinking skills.* Seattle, WA: Robbins/Layng & Associates.

Robbins, J. K. (1996). *TAPS for teachers.* Seattle, WA: Robbins/Layng & Associates.

Robinson, F. P. (1946). *Effective study.* New York: Harper.

Rosenshine, B. (1997). Advances in research on instruction. In J. W. Lloyd, E. J. Kameenui, and D. Chard (Eds.) *Issues in educating students with disabilities.* Mahwah, N.J.: Lawrence Erlbaum, 197–221.

Salvia, J., & Ysseldyke, J. E. (1991). *Assessment (5th ed)* Boston: Houghton Mifflin.

Samson, R. W. (1975). *Thinking skills: A guide to logic and comprehension.* Stamford, CT: Innovative Sciences.

Shaklee, B. D., Barbour, N. E., Ambrose, R., & Hansford, S. J. (1997). *Designing and using portfolios.* Boston: Allyn & Bacon.

Sherman, J. G., Ruskin, R. S., & Semb, G. B. (1982). *The personalized system of instruction: 48 seminal papers.* Lawrence, Kansas: TRI Publications.

Shinn, M. R. (1986). Does anyone really care what happens after the refer-test-place sequence: The systematic evaluation of special education effectiveness. *School Psychology Review, 15,* 49–58.

Shinn, M. R. (Ed.). (1989). *Curriculum-based measurement: Assessing special children.* New York: Guilford Press.

Shinn, M. R. (Ed.). (1998). *Advanced applications of curriculum-based measurement.* New York: Guilford Press.

Shinn, M. R., & Bamonto, S. (1998). Advanced applications of curriculum-based measurement: "Big ideas" and avoiding confusion. In M. R. Shinn (Ed.) *Advanced applications of curriculum-based measurement* (pp 1–31). New York: Guilford Press.

Shinn, M. R., & Habedank, L. (1992). Curriculum-based measurement in special education problem identification and certification decisions. *Preventing School Failure, 36(2),* 11–15.

Skinner, B. F. (1948). *Walden II.* New York: Macmillan.

Skinner, B. F. (1953). *Science and human behavior.* New York: Macmillan.

Skinner, B. F. (1957). *Verbal Behavior.* Englewood Cliffs, NJ: Prentice-Hall, Inc.

Skinner, B. F. (1968). *A technology of teaching.* New York: Appleton-Century-Crofts.

Skinner, B. F. (1969). *Contingencies of reinforcement: A theoretical analysis.* New York: Appleton-Century-Crofts.

Skinner, B. F. (1978). Designing higher education. In B. F. Skinner, *Reflections on behaviorism and society.* Engelwood Cliffs, N. J.: Prentice-Hall.

Stein, M., Silbert, J., & Carnine, D. (1997). *Designing effective mathematics instruction: A direct instruction approach (3ʳᵈ ed.).* Englewood Cliffs, NJ: Prentice-Hall.

Suchman (1966). *Teacher's guide: Inquiry development program in physical science.* Chicago, IL: Science Research Associates.

Sulzer-Azaroff, B., & Mayer, G. R. (1977). *Applying behavior analysis procedures with children and youth.* New York: Holt, Rinehart, & Winston.

Tiemann, P. W., & Markle, S. M. (1983; 1990). *Analyzing instructional content: A guide to instruction and evaluation.* Champaign, IL: Stipes.

Tishman, S., Perkins, D. N., & Jay, E. (1995). *The thinking classroom: Learning and teaching in a culture of thinking.* Needham Heights, MA: Allyn & Bacon.

Touchette, P. E. (1971). Transfer of stimulus control: Measuring the moment of transfer. *Journal of the Experimental Analysis of Behavior, 15*, 347–354.

Turner, J. C., Midgley, C., Meyer, D. K., Gheen, M., Anderman, E. M., Kang, Y., & Patrick, H. (2002). The classroom environment and students' reports of avoidance strategies in mathematics: A multimethod study. *Journal of Educational Psychology, 94*, 88–106.

von Glaserfeld, E. (1997). Amplification of a constructivist perspective. *Issues in Education: Contributions from Educational Psychology, 3*, 203–210.

Vygotsky, L. S. (1978). *Mind in society: The development of higher psychological processes.* Cambridge, MA: Harvard University Press.

Vygotsky, L. S. (1986). *Thought and language.* Cambridge MA: MIT Press.

Whimbey, A. (1975). *Intelligence can be taught.* New York: E.P. Dutton.

Whimbey, A., Johnson, M., Williams, E., & Linden, M. (1993). *Blueprint for educational change: Improving reasoning, literacies, and science achievement with cooperative learning.* Washington, DC: The Right Combination, Inc.

Whimbey, A. & Linden, M. J. (2001). *Teaching and learning grammar: The Prototype Construction Approach.* Chicago, IL: BGF Performance Systems, LLC.

Whimbey, A., & Lockhead, J. (1991). *Problem solving and comprehension.* Hillsdale, NJ: Lawrence Erlbaum.

Whimbey, A., & Lockhead, J. (1999). *Problem solving and comprehension (6th ed.).* Mahwah, New Jersey: Lawrence Erlbaum, Publishers.

Woods, D. R. (1998). The MPS program: The McMaster problem solving program. http://chemeng.mcmaster.ca/MPS/default1.htm. Retrieved February 2004.

INDEX